PRODUCTIVE CLASSROOM ASSESSMENT IN COLLEGE COURSES

A Practical Guide for Community College, College and University Faculty

Rick Stiggins

FOUNDER OF THE
ASSESSMENT TRAINING INSTITUTE
PORTLAND OR

ISBN: 0615827799
ISBN-13: 9780615827797

Forward

As I read Rick Stiggins' assessment guide for college professors I felt pulled by my multiple roles. For the last seven years I have been a university professor at a great institution in every respect except one, and that is fairly typical to higher education. Many of my university colleagues, brilliant in every other way, struggle with issues of pedagogy, especially at the onset of their careers. This is particularly true of graduate students assigned teaching duties for undergraduate classes. Recently I worked with a freshman on the verge of failing out of school. He had superior board scores, a slew of 5s on AP tests and wanted desperately to succeed. He came from a high school with excellent teachers with a deep understanding of teaching and appropriate use of assessment. Here was a really smart, hardworking kid on the way out the door and not quite understanding what happened.

Most of my colleagues are trained as researchers, as they should be. But a substantial portion of their time is spent teaching and advising. Many do have a keen understanding of lesson design and delivery. Indeed, I have seen some very effective teaching at the university level. Yet, I have also seen and heard of teaching that is not only ineffective, but not on track to improve. Discussion that does occur around effective teaching seems to end at lesson design and delivery. There is little discussion of assessment and the power it holds in actually improving teaching AND learning.

Rick Stiggins proposes that research based best practice be applied to college assessments. His goal is to achieve what he sees as "student academic self-efficacy", a term he borrows from

Albert Bandura, emeritus Professor of Psychology at Stanford. This mental state, Stiggins maintains, tends to establish the necessary conditions for future success, putting students on what he calls "winning streaks." This does not imply lowering standards in any way, but puts in place mechanisms that allow able students to meet high standards. Stiggins maintains that when students are not succeeding it becomes imperative that we and they understand why. If the college learner lacks the academic background or intellectual capability to succeed, then a change in direction is indicated. However, when such clear causes are not apparent, high-quality classroom assessments use effectively can point to the path to potential success thus rekindling learners' sense of confidence in themselves as learners. This can be accomplished by applying principles of assessment FOR learning; that is, by helping students see the target from the outset, compare their work to clear standards of excellence and learn to close the gap between the two.

Rick Stiggins' model is focused on student learning and five overlapping keys to productive classroom assessment. First, the assessor must be clear of purpose, asking why the assessment is needed: who will use it and how it will be used. Second, one must establish clear learning targets that are understood by all, especially the students. Third, we need to create high-quality assessments specifically designed to fit into the purpose/target context. Fourth, assessors must know how to clearly communicate results so that students can benefit from their own analysis of the assessment. Finally, the overarching concept in Stiggins' paradigm is to involve students as "players in the assessment process." Stiggins maintains "When students become involved in the self-assessment process during their learning and they have the opportunity to watch themselves ascending to ever-higher levels of proficiency, their confidence, motivation, engagement and achievement skyrocket." In other words, they begin to achieve what Bandura calls "self-efficacy".

I have seen this notion of assessment FOR learning work in a variety of setting; with elementary school children, in advanced high school mathematics classes and with my own graduate students. It requires a bit of a reset in ones one paradigm of instruction, but in the end, it seems to create a much deeper sense of ownership on the part of the students for their own success and a greater sense of accountability on the part of the teacher to a focus on clear and important learning targets.

I noted to begin with that I brought a range of roles to my study of the Stiggins book: former high school teacher, principal, superintendent and now university professor. There are two more; father of four and payer of tuition. Three of my own children have graduate degrees and, with our help, are paying down student loans for grad school. Our youngest is a senior in high school and considering a number of wonderful (and expensive) private universities, all of which will lead to several years of graduate school. She is well prepared, smart, hardworking and focused. I want her to be exposed to great minds AND great teaching at the college level. I can only hope that her professors will consider Rick Stiggins' ideas on assessment FOR learning when they design their courses.

Stephen Uebbing, Ph.D.
University of Rochester

Preface

I developed this guide in response to increasingly frequent requests from post-secondary faculty for advice on how to improve their course assessment practices. It details guidelines for sound classroom assessment practice that I have developed over the past 40 years from research and development at Michigan State, Minnesota, Stanford, Lewis and Clark College and the Northwest Regional Educational Laboratory. Over the past 20 of those years, my colleagues and I at the Assessment Training Institute (ATI) in Portland, OR created multimedia professional development programs in classroom assessment for K-12 teachers and school leaders. This guide transforms those universal standards of good practice for application in post-secondary classrooms.

The assessment strategies and tactics presented are adapted by permission of Pearson Education from our 2012 ATI in-service training program, *Classroom Assessment FOR Student Learning: Doing It Right, Using It Well (2nd Ed.)* and from my teacher preparation text, *An Introduction to Classroom Assessment FOR Student Learning (6th Ed).* The common-sense keys to quality assessment that are described here are applicable at all levels of education. They represent standards of sound practice will maximize the positive impact of assessment on student learning success.

In other words, the ideas offered herein will help educators at all levels understand how to use the assessment process and its results both to support learning (to help students learn more) and to verify or certify it (as in grading contexts). These two themes are woven evenly through the fabric of this presentation.

Historically in higher education in the USA has held few institutional or pedagogical norms for or concerns about the quality of course assessments. As a result, those assessments have been of uneven quality and professional development has rarely been available to help faculty members understand and learn to apply accepted standards of quality. Those standards are clearly framed herein for your consideration.

Similarly, there is no legacy in American education at any level of thinking addressing the classroom assessment process as an instructional intervention—as a way to promote greater student learning, not merely grade it. But the past 20 years have revealed stunning new ways to think about and use student-involved assessment during the learning process to encourage and promote greater academic success for our students. We know when and how to engage students in self-assessment as they make their way to achievement success. I also share those instructional/assessment strategies.

In other words, assessment should no longer be seen merely something attached to the end of teaching in order to derive test scores, grades, and GPA. Rather, it also can be used productively during instruction to promote greater student success.

Special note to the reader: Be advised that all proceeds from the sale of this book go directly to an endowment at Michigan State University whose mission is to promote the improvement of classroom assessment practices at all levels of education.

Rick Stiggins
Portland OR
June 2013

Table of Contents

Keys to Productive Assessment in College Classrooms

At any level of instruction, whether in primary grades or college classrooms, instructors can spend a quarter to a third of their available professional time engaged in assessment-related activities. So clearly assessment represents an essential foundation of effective instruction. It helps us decide what has and has not been learned and therefore what comes next in student learning and our instruction. Further, in many ways, assessment (the promise of being evaluated) drives student motivation and thus learning success. When it is done well, students benefit; but when it is done poorly student learning suffers. This guide is about how to do it correctly; that is, how to (1) gather accurate evidence of student learning, and (2) use the assessment process and its results *to benefit*, not merely measure, student learning. Students' well-being turns on their instructor's understanding and application of these two facets of assessment quality.

As educators, most of us began our teaching careers without having been given the opportunity to learn how to use assessment productively. This guide details the specific keys to quality we should have had the chance to learn. For those who are uncertain about the quality of your assessments, I provide criteria by which to evaluate those practices and ways to improvement them if needed. If, upon learning about those keys, the reader fears the worst about her or his assessment practices,

I provide concrete and immediate ways to improve them. Either way, I am quite certain readers will have their practices affirmed or enhanced through their study of this guide.

GUIDING PRINCIPLES

This presentation arises from four interrelated guiding principles:

- Instructors assess for two reasons: (a) to help us plan instruction based on student needs, and (b) to encourage students to study and learn.
- Critically important instructional decisions—that is, those that can enhance or inhibit learning—are made both by professors and by their students based predominately on the results of information gathered with classroom assessments
- The more accurate those assessment results and more clearly they are understood by their intended users, the better will be the quality of their decisions.
- The better the instructional decisions made by students and their teachers, the more effective will be the teaching and the greater will be the learning

In addition to these, I assert another overarching principle that deviates from common practice in many classrooms: I advocate open classroom assessment environments in which students are informed of achievement expectations in terms they can understand from the beginning of instruction. Students can hit any achievement target that they can see and that holds still for them. If they are left to guess about what they are supposed to learn, success becomes a random event.

In other words, I favor classroom assessment climates designed to maximize the number of students who succeed at meeting pre-established achievement expectations. I believe students should have continuous access to dependable information about the level of their learning success in relation to expectations. As I have said, I want assessment to *contribute to* student success, not merely monitor it. I want assessment be a cause of learning, not merely be a reflection of it. This requires accurate assessment results that are used productively in the service of both purposes.

KEYS TO ASSESSMENT QUALITY

There are five keys to productive assessment in college classrooms. Each one focuses on a particular dimension of quality by describing it in the form of a continuum from weak to strong. Three address the quality (accuracy) of the assessment itself, while two center on how to use that assessment most effectively. They are presented graphically in Figure 1.1 on the next page. This guide is structured to make these keys come alive for the reader.

Keys to Accurate Assessment Results

Key #1: Clear Purpose

The starting place for the creation of a quality assessment is a clear answer to the question, *why* am I conducting this assessment? The developer must begin with a sharply focused vision of who will use the results and how. If assessment is evidence gathering to inform instructional decisions in each context, it is vital to determine what instructional decisions hang in the balance. Without a sense of user(s) and use(s) of the assessment,

3

the developer cannot infer what kind of information it must produce. How does one build an assessment to provide information without knowing what information is needed?

In the chapters that follow, you will learn specific tactics and strategies for using course assessments for the purposes of (a) *support learning* (as an instructional intervention) and (b) *verify* that learning (in assigning grades, for example). Both are crucial to effective instruction.

Key 2: Clear Learning Targets

The second question one must address at the beginning of assessment development is, *what* student achievement is to be assessed? Without an established set of achievement expectations to be taught and learned, the author cannot properly focus test

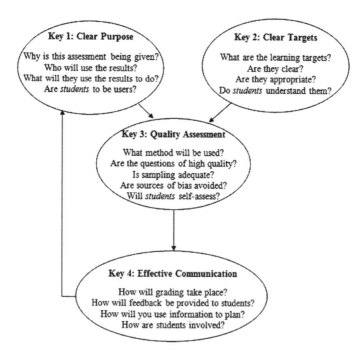

Figure 1.1 Keys to Quality Course Assessment

items or exercises and corresponding scoring procedures. That which is to be taught and learned is that which must be assessed.

Key 3: Quality Assessment

Once the assessment context is defined in terms of purpose (intended use of results) and learning target (what is to be assessed), then and only then can one answer the question, *how*, therefore, should I assess student learning? When I know why and what, then assessment design can begin. The creation of a quality assessment for any particular context requires the

- Selection of a proper assessment method for a specific context
- Development of a plan for sampling achievement
- Authoring of quality exercises and scoring guides,
- Elimination of relevant sources of bias that can distort results.

Details will be forthcoming in subsequent chapters on how to accomplish these things with great efficiency.

Keys to the Effective Use of Assessment

Key 4: Effective Communication of Results

When the high-quality assessment is completed it can be administered and it will produce dependable results. One must always bear in mind that the results have been gathered to serve an intended purpose. The next challenge is to deliver those results into the hands of the intended user(s) so they can inform the desired instructional decision(s). This requires *effective communication*—the transmission of those results in a timely and understandable manner to users prepared to act productively on them. The very highest-quality assessment yielding the most accurate of results is wasted if its results are mis-communicated. I will share specific guidelines for effective communication whether its purpose is to support or grade learning.

An Overarching 5th Key: Student-Involved Assessment During Learning

There is on more key to truly productive classroom assessment, and it centers on students as players in the assessment process. There is no bubble for this key in Figure 1.1. Rather, it is factored into the questions posed in each of the other four bubbles because, as you will learn, it crosses all other keys.

When students become involved in the self-assessment process *during their learning* and they have the opportunity to watch themselves ascending to ever-higher levels of proficiency, their confidence, motivation, engagement, and achievement skyrocket. Clearly, the most unique and innovative feature of this guide is that it details when and how to involve college students in self-assessment in productive ways in the service of their own success.

WHY A GUIDE TO COLLEGE CLASSROOM ASSESSMENT NOW?

Research on the potentially positive impact of high-quality classroom assessment on student learning is so compelling that it demands immediate dissemination and implementation. For example, we know that student success at learning increases as the accuracy of classroom assessment increases. As the quality of the assessment increases so does the dependability of the evidence it yields. As the accuracy of evidence increases, so will the quality of the decisions it informs. Most professors have not been given the opportunity to learn to assess dependably—thus, this book. That opportunity is at hand.

The same research also reveals that student achievement increases as the effectiveness of communication of results increases. Delivering assessment results to intended users in a timely and understandable manner while they are learning helps them stay on track and so improves that learning.

And, as students become involved in the assessment, record keeping, and communication process during their learning—that is, before they are to be held accountable for that learning—the greater will be their commitment to succeeding. This is true for all students but especially for struggling learners. Again, few instructors at any level of education have been given the opportunity learn to use assessment as a teaching tool to support learning.

Finally and from a different perspective, the accountability movement that has swept through public education over the past two decades has now arrived at the postsecondary level. It is increasingly the case that professors are being called upon to specify their achievement expectations up front and to provide dependable public evidence that their students are meeting those expectations; that is, evidence that the resources being invested in higher education institutions are being put to good use. To meet this emerging demand, faculties must develop their professional competence in assessment.

AN OVERVIEW OF THE PRESENTATION

Each of the chapters that follow addresses two the five keys to assessment quality described above. Chapter 2 focuses on the various purposes college course assessments can serve.

It highlights the various possible users and uses. Here I contrast and discuss the relationship between assessments used to help students learn more with assessments used to hold students accountable or to grade them. Both uses are important, but they are different. In this chapter, I will introduce the idea that students are very important data-based instructional decision makers too by discussing the decisions student typically make based on their interpretation of their own assessment results.

Chapter 3 addresses achievement expectations (learning targets) as a foundation for the development of quality assessment. It describes various kinds of achievement and the interrelationships among them. We cannot dependably assess learning targets we have not clearly and completely articulated. Chapter 3 also describes why and how to make those learning targets clear to the learners.

Chapter 4 presents part one of quality assessment design— the critical matter of selecting a proper assessment method for any given context. Professors have a wide variety of assessment options at our disposal, including selected response, written response, and performance assessment. The presentation shows readers how to connect each of these methods properly to achievement targets in order to obtain dependable results. Students also can be brought into the assessment development process for practice during the learning. I will discuss how.

Chapter 5 offers advice on what to do once the method is selected; that is, how to build classroom assessments out of high quality test items, essay exercises or performance tasks and associated scoring procedures.

Chapter 6 provides guidelines for the effective communication of assessment results in ways that both support learning (via student involvement) when that is the assessment purpose or to test the sufficiency of learning for accountability and grading purposes.

WE NEED A PARTNERSHIP

My approach to teaching lessons on sound assessment practice is simple and straightforward. I rely on clear description using simple, jargon-free prose. However, as I developed the guide I found that I had to face one big challenge. I am not able to offer the reader specific content-based examples to illustrate what my lessons would look like translated into your particular instructional context. It would be impractical, indeed impossible, for me to provide concrete illustrations of quality assessments spanning the immense array of academic subjects or levels of sophistication that post-secondary readers might expect. Obviously, I lack sufficient content expertise to do this. For this reason, I must rely on my very capable readers to infer how to bring these assessment ideas and suggestions to bear in your own academic contexts and disciplines in terms that make sense to you. This partnership is essential.

I urge you to experiment with your own specific applications of principles of sound practice described herein. It is only through this local individual or departmental practice that the strategies offered can come alive in any college context, community college context, including undergraduate or graduate study. In fact, Portland OR Community College created a course for faculty using a field trial version of this guide with very positive results. In that professional development context each faculty member had the opportunity to develop her or his own unique applications.

4

Understanding Various Uses of Assessment

This chapter explores the *purposes* for assessment: Key #1 in Figure 1-1. The starting place for the creation of a quality assessment in any context is a clear answer to the question, why am I assessing? In other words, who is going to use the results of this assessment and how? What specific instructional decisions hang in the balance? Without knowing the information needs of the intended user(s), it is impossible to develop assessments capable of delivering that information.

In the college classroom, the natural (indeed, almost automatic) response to an inquiry about why we assess is to measure the extent of student mastery of the required material in order to assign a grade at the end of the course. Assignments, quizzes, tests, and final exam contribute the evidence needed to calculate the composite index of each student's achievement need to determine their grade at the end of the semester.

While this reason for assessment certainly is dominant, if our goal is to maximize the effectiveness of instruction and to help students attain greatest learning success, then this uni-dimensional view of assessment's role is too restrictive. It's not inappropriate, it's insufficient. Obviously, classroom assessments can serve grading purposes. But they also can play many more and more productive roles.

In Chapter 1, we established that assessment is the process of gathering information to inform instructional decisions.

It is important to understand that, in the college classroom, important decisions are made both by instructors (like grade assignment) and by students themselves. In other words, the evidence of learning provided by assessments can serve either or both these users depending on the purpose. This chapter explores both teacher and student uses of assessment in college classrooms.

In the first chapter, I also pointed out that we assess to encourage students to try to learn—to motivate them to do the work that will result in the desired learning. This represents the affective or dispositional reason for assessing. Recent breakthroughs in research on the assessment/student motivation relationship make it possible for college instructors of today to tap powerful sources of motivation heretofore unavailable to our predecessors. This new application uses assessment to keep students constantly informed about and feeling in control of the evolution of their learning while it is happening. Our collective assessment heritage has paid little attention to the idea of students as assessment users—as users of their own assessment results and as makers of decisions about how to advance their own learning. But they are players in the assessment process and not merely as recipients of grades.

FACULTY USES OF ASSESSMENT

In additions to assessing to determine grades at the end of learning, postsecondary faculty also make instructional decisions during the learning that can impact the amount of learning and therefore the grades attained. Thoughtful classroom assessment can inform those decisions too. Here are several *course level* decisions that are likely to support learning if well made:

- Where should I begin instruction? A sharply focused pre-assessment can tell us where students are now, thus revealing what comes next in their learning. It also can reveal differences in students' starting places, thus permitting accommodation of those differences while planning instruction.
- How well is my instructional design and process working? Interim practice assessments during the teaching and learning (not for grading) can tell us if they are getting it or not in time to try new strategies if need be.

At the accountability level, a different set of questions emerges as important:

- What grade should I assign to each student at the end of the course? This requires a compilation of evidence of the extent to which each student met my pre-established achievement expectations.
- Are enough of my students mastering the academic achievement standards established for this program of study? This kind of accountability question can come up at program accreditation time. A high-quality final exam that reveals how each student performed in mastering each standard will inform judgments about the quality of my teaching as the semester unfolded over time.

STUDENT USES OF ASSESSMENT

In this case, it is useful to think about the classroom assessment process from the student's point of view. If their performance is at high levels and the indications are that they are succeeding, then the effect of ongoing classroom assessment can be to reinforce that impression for them and, therefore, to build their confidence in themselves as learners. Good assessment results promote optimism.

But what if a student is struggling and as a result, for them, pessimism rules? The easy response is to say, that's the student's problem. If they can't handle it, they don't belong here. They just need to try harder.

But, as it turns out, there is another answer that may be more productive in the long run. What if the instructor could replace pessimism in the student's mind with optimism by using the classroom assessment process during the learning to move these students from losing streaks to winning streaks? In recent years, understandings have emerged on how to use classroom assessment to rekindle their confidence that they do belong here and to build their motivation to succeed.

Before going further, I need to acknowledge that there are times in college contexts where students will find that they can't, in fact, handle the academic demands and really should move on. Their teachers should help them understand the evidence and respond appropriately. My concern, however, is for the student who can, in truth, achieve success but doesn't believe it. The healthier scenario in their case is to help them attain enough academic success ultimately to embrace that possibility and succeed in their chosen program of study. Then, they can decide stay or leave a particular program for reasons of a lack of interest or because they have found a more attractive field of study. As higher education instructors, our aspiration should be to minimize the number of students who erroneously infer that they can't succeed when, in fact, they can. This leads me to the idea of "assessment FOR learning."

Assessment to Support Learning

In the service of this success-oriented agenda, one must anticipate the questions students are asking about themselves based on their interpretation of their own academic records. In any particular course context, they ask:

- Can I learn this material or is it just beyond me?
- Is the learning worth the energy I must expend to attain it?
- Is trying worth the risk that I might fail in some embarrassing way?

Professors who want their students to answer these in the affirmative as much as possible can turn to what have come to be called "assessment FOR learning" principles and strategies for help.

Assessment FOR learning relies on student-involved self-assessment, record keeping, and communication to keep students believing that success is within reach if they keep trying. Chapter 1 identified four keys to quality with a fifth key permeating the others: student-involvement in assessment. To understand its connection to learning success, consider its relationship to the other four keys from Figure 1-1:

- The first is clear sense of *assessment purpose*—the users and uses of assessment. Students are near the top of the list of key classroom assessment users—see above some of the questions they strive to answer based on their interpretation of assessment results.
- The second key is a clear vision of the *achievement target*—the definition of what is to be learned and therefore assessed. By beginning instruction with a student-friendly version of

that target, we help students succeed. They can hit any target that they can see and that holds still for them.

- The third key is careful design of *quality assessments*. As it turns out, if we involve students *during their learning* in the development and use of practice assessments like those that they are to be held accountable, sense of control over their academic well-being can rise, along with their motivation and achievement. Ongoing self-assessment by students in a context where learning success dominates is an immensely powerful confidence builder.

- The fourth key is *effective communication* of assessment results. By providing students with a clear vision of the learning target, consistent access to accurate assessment of their learning, regular descriptive feedback (much of which they can learn to generate on their own with proper preparation) detailing how to do better the next time, and the opportunity to see changes in their own academic capabilities over time, one provides an assessment FOR learning environment that can contribute to a record of wonderful academic success.

Considered together, these strategies form a composite portrait of a classroom assessment environment in which students know what good work looks like from the beginning, learn to compare their work to that standard of excellence such that differences become clear to them, and learn to close the gap between the two.

To reiterate, one helps students see the target from the outset by providing a vision of the learning target from the beginning of the learning that students understand. Accompany this with actual samples of student work that reveal differences in quality, and a key foundation for confident learning is put in place. When I, the learner, have a clear sense of what is expected, I am more confident that I can deliver versus when I am guessing at what counts. You may remember that, in college, we used to call this psyching out the professor. Often we were guessing—guess wrong and suffer the consequences. My vision is of the opposite: the student's question should always be, can I hit the target, not what is that target.

To help students compare their work to the standard of excellence, we provide continuous access to descriptive feedback revealing how to improve, while transitioning as quickly as possible to a place where students are confident in applying the attributes of good work to their own and in generating their own descriptive feedback. From here, student and teacher can become partners in setting goals for what comes next in the learning. From then on, students can ease toward greater sense of internal control of their success. This is a confidence builder.

To help students close the gap between their current work and our model of excellence, instruction must help them improve the quality of their work one key attribute at a time, ultimately knowing that they will be able to merge all attributes when they have achieved learning success. The power of this strategy to encourage and build confidence resides in its potential to reveal to students increments in their achievement being attained steadily over time due to their own efforts. In short, their sense of their own academic self-efficacy builds.

Our Ultimate Goal for Our Students: Academic Self-Efficacy

A student's attitude has a direct and powerful impact on their learning. Our aspiration is to give each student a strong sense of control over her or his own academic well-being. Stanford professor Albert Bandura refers to this sense as self-efficacy. In the paragraphs that follow, he describes this continuum as a psychological construct. However, if the reader will think of this continuum in terms of the student's sense of control of learning success (academic self-efficacy, if you will), it will become clear that the consistent application of principles of assessment FOR learning can move students boldly toward the productive end:

> A strong sense of efficacy enhances human accomplishment and personal well-being in many ways. People with high assurance in their capabilities approach difficult tasks as challenges to be mastered rather than as threats to be avoided. Such an efficacious outlook fosters intrinsic interest and deep engrossment in activities. They set themselves challenging goals and maintain strong commitment to them. They heighten and sustain their efforts in the face of failure. They quickly recover their sense of efficacy after failures or setbacks. They attribute failure to insufficient effort or deficient knowledge and skills which are acquirable. They approach threatening situations with assurance that they can exercise control over them. Such an efficacious outlook produces personal accomplishments, reduces stress and lowers vulnerability...
>
> In contrast, people who doubt their capabilities shy away from difficult tasks which they view as personal threats. They have low aspirations and weak commitment to the goals they choose

to pursue. When faced with difficult tasks, they dwell on their personal deficiencies, on the obstacles they will encounter, and all kinds of adverse outcomes rather than concentrate on how to perform successfully. They slacken their efforts and give up quickly in the face of difficulties. They are slow to recover their sense of efficacy following failure or setbacks. Because they view insufficient performance as deficient aptitude it does not require much failure for them to lose faith in their capabilities. (p. 71)*

We help students build a strong sense of academic self-efficacy when we help them understand what success looks like and when we help them use practice assessment results to determine how to do better the next time. Assessments become far more than merely one-time events attached onto the end of the teaching. They become part of the learning process by keeping students posted on their progress and confident enough to continue striving.

SUMMARY

Under the heading of assessment purpose, college faculty use classroom assessment results to hold students accountable—to assign grades. This works to fulfill a communication purpose when the results accurately reflect student achievement. It also works as a motivator for those who are succeeding. It will tend to keep them confidence and striving for more success.

But if students are not succeeding it becomes imperative that we and they understand why. If the college learner lacks the academic background or intellectual capability to succeed, then a change in direction is indicated. However, when such clear causes are not apparent, classroom assessment can fulfill another purpose. It can point to the path to potential success thus rekindling learners' sense of confidence in themselves as learners. This can be accomplished by applying principles of assessment FOR learning; that is, by helping students see the target from the outset, compare their work to clear standards of excellence and learning to close the gap between the two.

---

* Bandura, A. (1994) Self-efficacy. In V.S. Ramachaudran (ed.) *Encyclopedia of human behavior.* Volume 4, 71-81. New York: Academic Press.

Clarifying Achievement Targets: A Foundation for Quality Assessment

It is only possible to develop a quality assessment when the developer starts with focused vision of the achievement is to be assessed. Here, we refer to Key #2: *Clear Learning Targets* in Figure 1-1. Those achievement expectations drive the questions to be posed and the manner in which examinee responses are to be evaluated. Whatever form those learning targets take, whether learning outcomes, instructional objectives, achievement standards, learning goals, competencies, academic proficiencies, or some other label, they focus instruction and frame the assessment challenge for college instructors.

This chapter is not about how to select those learning targets. I must leave that to you, the course instructor, because you are an expert in your field of study. Rather, the chapter is about how to think about achievement expectations in ways that (a) lay a solid foundation for quality assessment, and (b) help students attain a very high level of success in mastering them. We will address the attributes of useful learning targets, explore the benefits of clear targets for teacher and learner, and describe the various kinds of achievement that might be held as important in any particular college classroom.

KEY ATTRIBUTES OF QUALITY LEARNING TARGETS

Five key characteristics define achievement expectations capable of guiding quality instruction and properly focused course assessments:

1. Quality learning targets reflect the most up to date thinking in the professional literature in each field of study regarding the important learnings

To the extent possible, academic achievement expectations should reflect the best thinking of the leading experts of the field about the most important things for students to know and be able to do. If there are differences of opinion among reasonable content experts, then faculty departments must agree on the priorities to be reflected in the curriculum. But, whatever priorities are selected must have a solid basis in the literature of the relevant professional domain of study.

2. Quality achievement expectations are unambiguous and public for all to see from the beginning of instruction

When achievement standards are clear, all qualified faculty, will independently interpret and paraphrase them to mean essentially the same thing. This, as opposed to Rorshack inkblots that can be interpreted to mean anything anyone wants them to mean. Each achievement standard is sufficiently clear that those who are to teach them can provide actual samples of student work to illustrate different levels of proficiency.

Once stated in these terms, our expectations should be made public for all to see and understand, including faculty and students alike. As stated previously, students can hit any target that they can see and that holds still for them. Each faculty member's responsibility is to frame the learner's challenge, map a route to success, describe each to students, and coach them as the make that journey.

3. Achievement standards need to be organized in learning progressions that unfold logically over time in a manner consistent with the way students learn

The overall curriculum of a particular program of study should define ascending levels of proficiency that spiral through courses, mapping journeys to academic excellence. Each faculty member's course goals and objectives, therefore, arise directly from the learning that has come before and lead to that which will follow. The same is true within courses. That which is foundational or pre-requisite comes first and forms the basis for more advanced topics that follow.

Because of differences in the academic capabilities, students will ascend these progressions at different rates. Some will ascent quickly, others more slowly. The path to academic success doesn't change as a function of how fast one travels it. Each faculty must decide how and how much to accommodate these differences. Those accommodations cannot be made productively without deep faculty understanding of the learning progression into which their particular instruction fits.

If each instructor is free to select her or his content based merely on personal preference with no interaction with colleagues and thus no sense of a bigger picture, then through no fault of their own, students can be placed in the untenable position of being held accountable for things they can't learn due to a lack of prerequisites.

4. Quality learning targets are manageable in number and scope given the time and other resources available to teach and learn them.

Instructional time and other resources available to promote student learning are always limited. As mentioned, students vary in the rate at which they are capable of learning. And achievement expectations vary in the demands they place on teacher and learner. For all of these reasons, it is important to think through what one can expect of students and how much is too much.

5. Those who are to teach students to master achievement standards must, themselves, be competent masters of those standards.

As a teacher, I cannot dependably assess (let alone teach) achievement targets that I, myself, have not confidently and competently mastered. If one is not a master of the standards their students are to master and of the building blocks that provide mark student's journey up the scaffolding leading up to each, then both poor instructional and assessment decisions will result. This places students directly in harm's way through no fault of their own.

THE BENEFITS OF CLEAR AND APPROPRIATE TARGETS

The energy faculty members invest in defining clear about targets will pay big dividends at assessment time. First of all, they will provide a sharp focus and strong basis for for creating assessment exercises and scoring procedures. The result will be high-quality assessments. But in addition, here are some other valuable benefits will result.

Benefit: Control over one's own professional success

By placing a frame around expectations from the outset of instruction, faculty members set standard by which to gauge their own success as teachers. The better each instructor becomes at bringing students to mastery of delimited learning outcomes, the more successful he or she becomes as a teacher. The thoughtful use of classroom assessment can help with this. If one succeeds as a teacher and students hit the target, she or he deserves an acknowledgement of that success. If students fail to hit the target, then teachers should want to know it too so they can investigate why they failed.

There are several possible reasons why students might not have learned:

1. They lacked the prerequisites necessary for success
2. The instructor didn't understand the target to begin with, and so could not convey it effectively
3. Instructional methods, strategies, and materials used were inadequate
4. Students weren't motivated to strive for success
5. Some force(s) outside of classroom and beyond the instructor's control (a personal emotional upset, for example) interfered with and inhibited learning.

The actions one takes in the face of such failure will vary depending on the cause and one cannot select an action without knowledge of the cause. For example and from an instructor's personal point of view, if my students lacked prerequisites (reason 1), I need to rethink entrance requirements and get with my colleagues who teach at preliminary levels of instruction to be sure our respective curricula mesh. If I am not qualified to teach the targets in question or rely on an inadequate instructional approach (reasons 2 or 3), I have to take responsibility for very important professional development or stop teaching those targets. Similarly, if my students lack confidence or motivation (reason 4), I may need to investigate why and discover better motivational strategies. And finally, if reason 5 applies (forces beyond my control), then I need to understand the strengths and limitations of my classroom actions and strive to be the best I can be within that context.

In any event, my success turns on my being willing to take the risk of asking why my students didn't learn. This requires that I (1) gather dependable information about student success or failure using my own high-quality classroom assessments, and (2) becoming enough of a classroom researcher to try to uncover the causes of any student failure. If I as a teacher simply bury my head in the sand and blame my students for not caring or not trying, I may doom them to long-term failure for reasons beyond their control. If it is my fault or if I can contribute to fixing the problem in any way, I must act accordingly.

Benefit: Student Academic Self-efficacy

The research cited earlier is clear: students benefit from seeing the target from the beginning of instruction. If I can help them understand these expectations, I set them up to take responsibility for their own success. The attitudinal and motivational implications of this for students can be immense.

For instance, let's say you are a student facing a big test. A great deal of material has been covered. You have no idea what will be emphasized on the test. You study your heart out but, alas, you concentrate on the wrong material. Nice try, but you fail. How do you feel when this happens? Are you feeling in control of your own academic well-being or not? How are you likely to behave the next time a test comes up under these same circumstances?

Now, consider facing that same test having had a different experience: a great deal of material has been covered, but your teacher, who has a complete understanding of the field, points out the parts that are critical for you to master. Thus, you study in a very focused manner, concentrating on the important material and its application. Your result is a high score on the test. Good effort—you succeed. Again, how do you feel? What impact will this experience have on your sense of self-efficacy? How are you likely to behave the next time a test comes up under these circumstances?

Given clear requirements for success, students are better able to gauge the appropriateness of their own preparation and thus gain control over their own academic well-being. Students who feel in control of their own chances for success are more likely to care and to strive for excellence.

Benefit: Greater Assessment Efficiency

Clear achievement targets can speed assessment development. Here's how: Any assessment is a sample of all the questions we could have asked if the test were infinitely long. But because time is always limited, we can never probe all important dimensions of achievement in final exams, for example. So we sample, asking as many questions as we can within the allotted time. A sound assessment asks a representative set of questions, allowing us to infer a student's performance on the entire domain of material from that student's performance on the shorter sample. If we have set clear limits on our valued target, then we have set a clear sampling frame. This allows us to sample with maximum efficiency and confidence; that is, to gather just enough information on student achievement without wasting time over-testing. When I have a clear sense of the desired ends, I can use the assessment methods that are most efficient for the situation.

Benefit: More Accurate Classroom Assessments

In subsequent chapters, you will study several assessment methods, concentrating on when to use each and how to use each well. Some methods work well with certain kinds of achievement targets but not with others. In addition, some methods produce achievement information more efficiently than do others. Skillful classroom assessors match methods to targets so as to produce a maximum amount of information with a minimum invested assessment time. This match cannot be made without clear learning targets.

TYPES OF LEARNING OUTCOMES

Our team at the Assessment Training Institute has researched and analyzed the task demands of classroom assessment. As part of that work we sought a way to categories learning targets in ways that seemed to make sense to teachers. We collected, studied, categorized, and tried to understand the various kinds of valued expectations reflected in teachers' classroom activities and assessments. The following types of achievement targets emerged as important, both as independent outcomes and in terms of their relationship to one another:

- *Knowledge*—mastery of content, where mastery includes both knowing and understanding it

- *Reasoning*—the ability to use that knowledge and understanding to figure things out and to solve problems
- *Performance Skills*—proficiency in doing something where it is the overt behavior or process that is important, such as playing a musical instrument, reading aloud, speaking in a second language, or using psychomotor skills
- *Products*—the ability to create tangible products, such as term papers, scientific models, and art products, that meet certain standards of quality

These categories are useful in thinking about classroom assessment, we decided, because they subsume all possible targets, are easy to understand, relate to one another in significant ways, and (now here's an important part!) have clear links to different methods of assessment. But before we discuss assessment, let's more thoroughly understand these categories of achievement targets.

Knowledge Targets

All academic competence arises from a foundation of knowledge. One can't speak a new language unless and until one has learned its vocabulary and syntactic structure. In the absence of sciences knowledge, scientific inquiry will remain unproductive. In is impossible to read with comprehension material we don't already know something about; in fact, communication of any sort banks of common knowledge of vocabulary.

Because factual, conceptual, or procedural knowledge is always prerequisite to mastery of the other three more complex achievements, it is part of any teacher's job to be sure students gain control of the key content. In the service of fulfilling this mission in the college classroom, three insights about mastery of content knowledge become important:

First, knowing something is not the same as understanding it. To understand content, students need to see how it fits into the larger schema of the academic discipline they are studying. Merely knowing but not understanding leaves any learners unable to make use of what they have learned. Memorizing the multiplication tables without understanding the underlying mathematical concept does not make that knowledge useful. Learning to mimic French phrases cannot lead to effective communication. But knowing and understanding the meaning of such phrases will. Therefore, as a course instructor/assessor, I must know and understand what I expect my students to master. Further, I must be prepared to assess my students' understanding of what they claim to know.

Second, in this information age, the world does not operate merely on facts stored in our brains. I am every bit as much a master of content if I know where to find it as if I know it outright. This way of knowing has become crucial in our information age. This "knowledge" category targets includes both those targets that students must learn outright to function within an academic discipline (core facts, concepts, relationships within structures of knowledge, principles, accepted procedures) and those targets they tap as needed through their use of reference resources. Each presents its own unique classroom assessment challenges to be discussed later.

Third, there are many ways to come to know and understand something: I can rehearse and thus memorize it. I can come to know because I figured it out and the resulting insight leaves an indelible impression. I can come to know because frequent use of certain knowledge over the long haul leaves its residue. Give students a list to memorize and in the end they will know it. If that list bears useful information and knowing is accompanied by understanding, important learning has occurred. Put learners in a situation where they must use the same body of knowledge repeatedly, and habits of use eventually will entitle them to learn it and not to have to look it up every time. Present students with a novel problem that force me to put together for the first time two pieces of knowledge previously assembled in order to find a solution, and once they figure it out, that solution becomes part of their knowledge. All are potentially useful ways of learning, if knowing is accompanied by understanding.

Reasoning Targets

Asking students to master content for the sake of knowing it and for no other reason is virtually never the college instructor's aspiration for students. Rather, we want students to be able to use their knowledge and understanding to reason, to figure things out, to solve certain kinds of problems. For example, one might want students to

- *Analyze* and solve problems in math
- *Compare* current or past political events or leaders
- Use science knowledge to *reason inductively and deductively* in science to find solutions
- *Evaluate* opposing positions on social and political issues

Those who hold such targets as valuable must define precisely what is meant by reasoning and problem-solving proficiency. Exactly what does it mean to reason "analytically", for example, in a case study context in a business manage course? It means that one can take things apart, at least mentally, and

31

know how the parts come together to form a functional whole. But what is the difference between doing that well and doing it poorly? That's the key learning and assessment question. What does it mean to reason "comparatively"? We do this when we think about similarities and differences. But when and how is it relevant to do in a finance context? What does it mean to categorize, synthesize, to reason inductively or deductively? What *is* critical or evaluative reasoning, anyway? How will one know if students are doing it well?

Not only must instructors be clear about their answers to these questions; that is, the underlying structure of these patterns of reasoning that underpin their academic discipline, but we must help students understand and take possession of them too. And, of course, college faculty members must be able to translate their valued reasoning pattern into classroom assessment exercises and scoring procedures in order to evaluate student learning; that is, we must understand ourselves what it means to do it well or poorly. The assessment challenge lies in knowing the difference. Success in helping students learn to monitor the quality of their own reasoning—a critical part of lifelong learning—is to *help them understand the difference.*

Performance Skill Targets

On occasion, expectations go beyond mental operations into contexts in which the measure of attainment is students' ability to demonstrate that they can perform or behave in a certain way. Examples include physical education, artistic, or dramatic performance, communication in a foreign language, and public speaking.

In all of these cases, success lies in actually *doing* it well. The assessment challenge lies in being able to define in clear terms, using words, examples, or both, what it *means* to do it well—to read fluently, work productively as a team member, or carry out the steps in a lab experiment. To assess well, we must provide opportunities for students to show their skills, so we can observe and evaluate while they are performing.

To perform skillfully, one must possess the foundational procedural knowledge and reasoning proficiency needed to figure out what skills are required. Further, skillful performance must combine with foundational knowledge and reasoning proficiency to create quality products (the next kind of achievement defined below). In this way, performance skills represent an end in and of themselves as well as a building block for other competencies. For example, one cannot produce a quality piece of writing (a product) unless I have handwriting or computer keyboarding proficiency (performance skills) *and* the ability to think about the topic in ways that permit me to write fluently and coherently. One cannot deliver an effective spontaneous speech (skill) unless I know something about the subject and can figure out what needs to be said about that topic at this moment. It is critical that we understand that, in this category, the student's performance objective is to put all the foundational knowledge and reasoning proficiencies together and to be skillful. This is precisely why achievement-related skills often represent complex targets requiring quite sophisticated assessments. Success in creating products—the next kind of target—virtually always hinges on the ability to perform some kinds of skills. Performance skills underpin product development.

Product Development Targets

Yet another way for students to succeed academically in some contexts is by developing the capacity to create products that meet certain standards of quality. These represent tangible entities that are created by the performer, and that present evidence in their quality that the student has mastered foundational knowledge, requisite reasoning and problem-solving proficiencies, and specific production skills.

Examples include research or term papers, scientific apparatus properly assembled, visual arts creations, and video, audio, or software products.

In all cases, success for the student lies in creating products that possess certain key attributes when completed. The assessment challenge is to be able to define clearly and understandably, in writing and/or through example, what those attributes are. We must be able to specify exactly how high- and low-quality products differ, and we must be prepared to express those differences in student-friendly language.

Student-Friendly Targets

To repeat: students can hit any target that they can see and that holds still for them. But if the target is missing, vague, or keeps moving, success remains beyond reach. So each faculty member's responsibility is to bring their expectations alive for their students from the beginning of instruction.

Often, this is not a challenging task. It can be as simple as providing an overview outline of the content to be mastered in a particular course or ongoing program of study—differentiating, of course, between that content that students are to learn out right and that which needs to be accessible to the student through reference sources if and when they need it.

Reasoning patterns, performance skills, and quality products can be more challenging to covey early in the learning. In most contexts, sharing examples or models of high-quality work can do the trick. In fact, it is often helpful to share examples of poor quality work too, so students can begin to understand the differences.

SUMMARY

One cannot dependably assess (let alone teach) learning targets that one has not clearly, completely, and appropriately defined according to the best current thinking of the field and confidently mastered themselves. So achievement expectations form one of the foundations of quality assessment.

The benefits of clear targets are legion. They set the parameters of, and therefore hold the promise of maximizing, assessment quality. But more importantly, the define the terms of both student and instructor success.

The building blocks of academic competence call for the mastery of content knowledge, the ability to use that knowledge to reason and solve problems, the development of performance skills and the ability to create products that meet standards of quality.

Matching Achievement Targets to Assessment Methods

Having established that any assessment must be created to fit into the context of a particular purpose and learning target(s), next comes the task of selecting an assessment method and the creation of the assessment itself. We are moving on the *Key #3: Assessment Design* in Figure 1-1.

First, an overview of this process: In all cases, productive assessment design and development requires the effective management four specific design features. The developer must to the following in this order:

1. Select a proper assessment method
2. Plan to sample student achievement effectively
3. Build the assessment of high-quality ingredients
4. Anticipate how to avoid all relevant sources of bias that can distort the results

This chapter is about the first feature only: selecting a proper assessment method. Chapter 5 will provide guidelines for addressing the remaining features.

College faculty members have four basic assessment methods at their disposal, all of which are familiar:

- Selected response assessment
- Written response or essay assessment
- Performance assessment
- Direct personal interaction or communication with students

I will describe them and then discuss the alignment of each to the kinds of achievement targets described in the previous chapter (knowledge, reasoning, performance skills, and products).

Perhaps the most important understanding to derive from this chapter is the fact that these assessment methods are not interchangeable. Some work well in some learning outcomes but are to be avoided in others. Don't adopt any single method as a favorite for use all the time, as contexts may arise where it cannot accurately reflect the valued learning outcomes. Forcing an inappropriate assessment method into places where it doesn't belong will lead to the mis-measurement of student learning.

Table 4-1 provides a framework within which to think about how each of these four assessment methods can be aligned with the four kinds of achievement targets. Each cell of the table matches a method with a target type. Some cells capture strong alignments that we can use to advantage. Some matches just cannot work and are to be avoided. I will explain why.

Table 4.1

Matching Assessment Methods to Learning Targets

Type of Learning Target Method:	Selected Response	Written Response	Performance Assessment	Personal Communication
Knowledge				
Reasoning				
Performance Skills				
Products				

THE RANGE OF AVAILABLE ASSESSMENT METHODS

The assessment methods available to educators today are the same as they have been for decades: respondents select the best answer, write a quality answer, perform according to certain criteria, or reveal their achievement in verbal interaction with their teacher. Each has its own utility.

Selected Response Assessment

This category includes all of the "objectively scored" paper and pencil test formats—that is, answers are right or wrong. Respondents are asked a series of questions, each of which is accompanied by a range of alternative responses. Their task is to select either the correct or the best answer from among the options. The index of achievement derived is the number questions answered correctly.

Format options within this category include the following:

- multiple-choice items
- true/false items
- matching exercises
- short answer fill-in items

Fill-in-the-blank items do require a response originating from within a respondent's mind, but we include it in this category because it calls for the respondent to select a very brief answer from a limited array of options that is scored right or wrong.

Written Response or Essay Assessment

In this case, respondents are provided with an exercise that calls for them to prepare an original written answer. Respondents might answer questions about content knowledge or provide an explanation of the solution to a complex problem. The examiner reads this original written response and evaluates it by applying specified scoring criteria.

Evidence of achievement is seen in the conceptual substance of the response (i.e., ideas expressed and the manner in which they are tied together). In this case, the student's score is determined by the number of points attained out of a number of available points.

Performance Assessment

In one version of performance assessment, respondents actually carry out a specified activity to demonstrate a performance capability under the watchful eye of an evaluator. In the other version the student submits a piece of work to the evaluator who observes and evaluates a product to judge level of achievement demonstrated.

So performance assessments can be based either on observations of respondents as they are demonstrating some behavior (such as giving a public presentation) or based on the products created as a result of having performed (a research paper). In this sense, like essay assessments, performance assessments consist of two parts: a performance task or assignment and a set of scoring criteria.

Personal Communication as Assessment

One of the most common ways teachers at all levels gather information about student achievement during their learning is to talk with them. Typically, this takes the form of questions posed and answered during instruction. But it also can take the form of oral exams in the accountability or grading context. The examiner listens to responses and either (1) judges them right or wrong if correctness is the criterion, or (2) makes subjective judgments according to some continuum of quality.

This may represent one of the most important forms of assessment available to those who seek to support learning, such as when one relies on questions during instruction to lead students to important inferences, interviews or conferences intended to discover and remedy misunderstandings, and listening during class discussions to uncover and immediately address misconceptions or acknowledge learning successes.

Personal communication is a very flexible means of assessment that we can bring into play literally at a moment's notice. While it certainly is not as efficient as some other options, by asking a student a carefully crafted set of follow up questions an instructor can probe achievement far more deeply than can the other alternatives.

When using oral examinations as part of the grading process, there are very important quality control criteria to keep in mind. We will cover those in Chapter 5.

MATCHING METHODS WITH TARGETS

Note that three of the four assessment methods described call for students to develop complex original responses. They require extended written responses, demonstrate complex performance skills, create multidimensional products, or participate in one-on-one communication, all of which take more time to administer and certainly more time to score than, say, true/false test items. Thus, if the amount of assessment time is held constant, selected response assessments can yield a broader sample of achievement (we can administer more items) per unit of assessment time.

Given this fact, you might ask, why not just use selected response all the time? The reason is that selected response assessment formats cannot validly depict all of the kinds of achievement we expect of our students. Different kinds of assessment methods align well with some kinds of achievement targets and not well with others.

Your objective, given a choice of methods, is to identify the most efficient (most valid evidence per unit of time) that fits the target/decision context. As it turns out, the recipes for creating these blends are not complicated.

As specified above in Table 4-1, one can blend four kinds of learning outcomes with the four methods to create a table depicting strong and weak matches of targets to methods. The result is both understandable and practical. Table 4.2 presents brief descriptions of the various matches.

Target #1: Assessing Knowledge and Understanding

Here is how the available assessment methods align with knowledge and understanding targets:

Selected Response

Selected response, objective paper and pencil tests, can be used to measure student mastery of knowledge of facts, concepts, generalizations and procedures. But remember, these tests are made up of independent items that test mastery of disconnected elements of knowledge of history, science, literature, foreign language vocabulary, and the like. When assessing knowledge of more complex relationships among those elements, other assessment methods may be more useful. More about that later.

These tests are efficient in that we can administer large numbers of multiple-choice or true/false test items per unit of testing time. Thus, they permit us to sample widely and draw relatively confident inferences about achievement status from the content sampled. For this reason, when the target is knowledge mastery, selected response formats fit nicely into the resource realities of most classrooms.

But remember, even with this most traditional of all assessment methods, things can go wrong. Poorly written items, non-representative sampling of the achievement domain, or items insensitive to students' different cultural experiences can lead to mis-measurement. We will address those in Chapter 5.

Written Response or Essay

When the domain of knowledge is defined, not as elements in isolation, but rather as important relationships among elements, larger inclusive concepts, or broader more complex generalizations—in other words, where the knowledge to be mastered is organized in complex ways—we can test student mastery by having them portray their knowledge using an extended written essay format. Examples of

Table 4.2

Aligning Learning Targets with Appropriate Assessment Methods

TARGET TO BE ASSESSED	*ASSESSMENT METHOD*			
	SELECTED RESPONSE	**ESSAY**	**PERFORMANCE ASSESSMENT**	**PERSONAL COMMUNICATION**
KNOWLEDGE MASTERY	Multiple choice, true/false, matching, and fill-in can sample mastery of discrete elements of knowledge	Essay exercises can tap understanding of relationships among elements of knowledge	Not a good choice for this target; three other options are preferred	Can ask questions, evaluate answers and infer mastery–but a time-consuming option
REASONING PROFICIENCY	Can assess understanding of basic patterns of reasoning	Written descriptions of complex problem solutions can provide a window into reasoning proficiency	Can watch students solve some problems and infer about reasoning proficiency	Can ask student to "think aloud" or can ask follow up questions to probe reasoning
SKILLS	Can assess mastery of the knowledge prerequisites to skillful performance–but cannot rely on these to tap the skill itself		Can observe and evaluate skills as they are being performed	Strong match when skill is oral communication proficiency; also can assess mastery of knowledge prerequisite to skillful performance
ABILITY TO CREATE PRODUCTS	Can assess mastery of knowledge prerequisite to the ability to create quality products–but cannot use these to assess the quality of products themselves		A strong match; can assess; (a) proficiency in carrying out steps in product development, and (b) attributes of the product itself	Can probe procedural knowledge and knowledge of attributes of quality products–but not product quality

larger information chunks we might ask students to know are the causes of migration or the principles of energy conservation.

In this case, we sample with fewer exercises, because each exercise requires longer response times and provides relatively more information than any single selected response item would.

Further, essay assessments present a more complex scoring challenge, and not just in terms of the time it takes. Because one subjectively judges response quality, versus merely counting it right or wrong, rater bias can creep in if we are not cautious. We address this and other sources of potential bias in Chapter 5.

Performance Assessment

When it comes to the use of performance assessment to detect mastery of content knowledge, things quickly become complicated. This match is not always a strong one. To see why, consider a brief example.

Let's say we ask a student to complete a rather complex repair of a piece of technical equipment in order to determine if the student understands the equipment. If the student succeeds, the equipment will work properly. So this is an instance of product-based performance assessment. Success turns on attributes of the final product. If the student successfully completes the repair and the piece works properly, then we know that she possesses the prerequisite knowledge of equipment assembly and operations needed to both identify and solve the problem. In this case, the match between performance assessment and assessment of mastery of knowledge is a strong one.

However, to understand the potential problem with this match, consider the instance in which the student failed to produce functioning equipment. Was her failure due to lack of knowledge? Or did she possess the required knowledge but not use it properly to identify the problem (a flaw in reasoning)? Or did the student possess the knowledge and reason productively, but fail because of inept use of repair tools (a performance skill problem)? At the time the student fails to perform successfully, we just don't know.

In fact, we cannot know the real reason for failure unless and until we follow up the performance assessment by asking some questions to find out the cause. In short, unless we turn to one of the other assessment methods to gather more evidence, we can't dependably assess achievement. But if our initial goal simply was to determine if she had mastery of that prerequisite content knowledge, why go through all this hassle? Why not just ask—that is, turn to one of the other three options from the outset?

Also understand that consideration of the purpose for the assessment represents an important consideration here. As the assessor, if my reason for assessing is to certify repair technicians, I don't care why the student failed. But if I am a teacher whose job is to help students learn to perform, unless I know why this student failed, I have no way to help her perform better in the future.

Personal Communication

The final option for assessing mastery of knowledge is direct personal communication with students, for example, by asking questions and evaluating answers. This is a good match across all contexts, especially with limited amounts of knowledge to be mastered, few students to be assessed, and in contexts where we need not store records of performance for long periods of time.

Obviously, this is a time- and labor-intensive assessment method. So if the domain of knowledge to assess is large, the assessor is faced with the need to ask a large number of questions to each student to sample it appropriately. That may not fit the resource realities in a particular contextm. Further, if the number of students to be assessed is large, this option may not allow enough time to sample each student's achievement representatively. And, if accurate records of performance must be kept over an extended period of time, written records will be needed for each student over a broad sample of questions. This, too, eats up a lot of time and energy. This option is inefficient.

Therefore, assessment via personal communication works best in those situations when teachers are checking student mastery of critical content during instruction in order to make quick, ongoing adjustments as needed. Further, sometimes with some students in some contexts, it is the only method that will yield accurate information. For various reasons, some students just cannot or will not participate in the other forms of assessment, such as those who experience debilitating evaluation anxiety, have difficulty reading English, have severe learning or communication disabilities, or simply refuse to "test."

Target #2: Assessing Reasoning Proficiency

In the previous chapter, we established that virtually every academic discipline defines itself, at least in part, in terms of valued patterns of reasoning—ways of using knowledge to solve problems. For example, one is *evaluative* or *critical thinking*, or the ability to make judgments and defend them through application of criteria. In newspapers, movie or restaurant critics evaluate based on their standards of quality. So too can students evaluate the quality of a piece of literature or the strength of a scientific argument by learning to apply certain criteria of quality or standards of excellence. This is evaluative reasoning in action.

Another commonly valued pattern across disciplines is *analytical* reasoning, the ability to break things down into component parts and to see how the parts work together. Yet another pattern involves using foundational knowledge to *compare and contrast* things, to infer similarities and differences.

Within disciplines, valued reasoning patterns carry different labels and levels of complexity, such as algorithmic math problem solving, the discipline of scientific inquiry, the composition of original text in writing, or reading complex material with comprehension.

As I already have declared, I will not attempt to define all such learning targets as they might play out across the various academic disciplines throughout post-secondary education. Indeed, I would be incapable of doing so. However, it is the responsibility of each and every instructor to determine if such expectations are relevant in her or his classroom. If they are, then they must be defined and shared with students from the beginning of instruction. And obviously, each instructor must, themselves, become a competent master of those reasoning patterns. Without that foundation, effective classroom assessment (let alone sound instruction) will remain beyond reach.

Assuming that those conditions are met, then how does one assess such reasoning targets? All four assessment methods can come into play here, depending on the nature of the reasoning.

For example, selected response exercises can reveal if students can reason effectively. We can use them, for example, to see if students can analyze literatures, compare pieces of literature, or draw inferences or conclusions in that academic arena. Consider the following illustration from a reading assessment context:

When that assessment poses novel questions immediately after reading, it asks students to dip into their newly formed knowledge base and use it to reason in order to ferret out the right answer. New questions demand the demonstration of reasoning proficiency on the spot versus reliance on memory of the solutions to previously solved problems. Students who see themselves as becoming increasingly proficient at responding to questions like these become increasingly confident interpreters of literature or whatever form of reasoning is valued.

It is surprising how many educators believe that selected response exercises can test only recall of content knowledge. While multiple-choice formats certainly can do that very well, they also can tap important reasoning proficiencies such as simple reasoning processes like comparison, analysis, and inductive or deductive inferences where there is one correct or best answer.

There are limits, however. *Evaluative reasoning*—the ability to express and defend a judgment, opinion, or point of view—cannot be tested using multiple-choice or true/false items because this kind of reasoning requires at least a presentation of the defense. Answers are not merely right or wrong—they vary in quality. Essay, performance assessment, or personal communication methods are needed to present that defense.

In a similar sense, problems that are multifaceted and complex, involving several steps, the application of several different patterns of reasoning, and/or several problem solvers working together, as real-world problems often do, demand more complex assessment methods.

Written Response or Essay

This represents an excellent way to assess student reasoning and problem solving. Student writing provides an ideal window into student thinking. Instructors can devise highly challenging exercises that ask students to analyze, compare, draw complex inferences, evaluate, or use some combination of these proficiencies, depicting their reasoning in written form.

Of course, as mentioned above, to evaluate the quality of student responses to such exercises one must understand the pattern of reasoning required and be able to detect its presence in student writing. This calls for exercises that really do ask students to reason through an issue or figure something out on the spot, not just regurgitate something that they learned earlier. And these exercises must be accompanied by clear and appropriate scoring criteria that reflect sound reasoning, not just content mastery.

Performance Assessment

Once again, here we have another excellent option that is applicable across academic contexts. Observing students as they act to solve problems in a science lab, for example, can inform inferences about their reasoning proficiency. To the extent that they carry out proper procedures or find solutions when stymied, they reveal their ability to reason. When we watch students use computer software to accomplish something that they haven't done before, we can literally see their reasoning unfolding in their actions.

However, drawing conclusions about reasoning proficiency on the basis of the quality of student products can be tricky. If performance is weak, did the student fail to perform because of a lack of foundational knowledge, failure to reason productively, or lack of motivation? As previously stated, without follow-up assessment by other means, we just don't know. If we don't follow-up with supplemental assessment, and thereby infer the wrong cause of failure, at the very least our remedy is likely to be inefficient. We may waste valuable time re-teaching material already mastered or teaching reasoning skills already developed.

Personal Communication.

One of the strongest matches between target and assessment method in Table 4.1 is between personal communication and student reasoning. Teachers can do any or all of the following:

- Ask questions that probe the clarity, accuracy, relevance, depth, and breadth of reasoning.
- Have students ask each other questions and listen for evidence of sound reasoning.
- Have students reason out loud, describing their thinking as they confront a problem.
- Have students recount their reasoning processes.
- Ask students to evaluate each other's reasoning.
- Simply listen attentively during class discussions for evidence of sound, appropriate reasoning.

Just talking informally with students can reveal so much, when we know what we're looking for! However, with this method, it will always take time to carry out the assessment and to keep accurate records of results.

Target #3: Assessing Mastery of Performance Skills

When the assessment context demands that we find out if students can demonstrate performance skills, such as play a role in a dramatic performance, fluently speak in a second language, effectively give a formal speech, demonstrate physical skill or agility and the like, there is just one way to assess: direct observation and evaluation of performance. This requires performance assessment using evaluation criteria reflective of the keys to success.

In addition, when the learning target takes the form of verbal proficiency or oral communication skills, such as speaking a foreign language then, obviously, personal communication is the highest-fidelity assessment option.

Target #4: Assessing Proficiency at Creating Products

The same limitations discussed for performance skills assessment apply here. If our assessment goal is to determine whether students can create a certain kind of achievement-related product, there is no other way to assess than to have them actually create one. In fact, performance assessment represents the only means of direct assessment. The best test of the ability to create an art product is to observe and judge the real product. The best test of the ability to set up a scientific apparatus properly is the completed arrangement of equipment. The best evidence of the ability to write a quality term paper is the finished paper.

SUMMARY

College faculties have a wide array of powerful assessment methods at our disposal. One can ask direct questions and evaluated the correctness of the student's response, ask students to compose text to describe their academic competence, present a task that students to demonstrate a particular skill or create a particular product and observe and evaluate the student's response, or talk with them directly to discern their level achievement. But these assessment methods are not interchangeable. Some work well with some kinds of achievement but not with others. Part of classroom assessment literacy lies in knowing what methods to use when.

But the very good news, as you will see, is that all of them can be used either (1) during instruction with student involvement to help students learn more, or (2) at the end of learning to document student achievement for accountability purposes.

Developing Quality Assessments

Thus far, we have established that we assess to help both faculty and students make specific instructional decisions that will help students master pre-set learning outcomes. In the previous chapter, we decided that this is doable only if we select proper assessment methods given the learning target to be assessed.

Once that method is selected, work can begin on the creation of the assessment itself. The assessment development process unfolds in three phases. In all cases, one must:

- Formulate a sampling plan
- Author the test items, tasks, exercises and scoring keys and guides that will make up the assessment itself
- Anticipate and eliminate sources of bias that can distort results

Regarding *sampling*, any test is composed of a subset or sample of all possible questions. Practicality necessitates asking a limited, but representative, set questions from which the assessor infers how the student would have performed on that theoretical comprehensive examination. The challenge is to gather enough evidence to lead to a confident conclusion about student learning without wasting time gathering too much. In other words, the sampling goal is to create the highest-resolution picture of that valued target one can while relying on the smallest possible sample; maximum information for minimum cost.

Once the sampling plan is final, it must be filled out with *high-quality test items or exercises and scoring procedures.* If it is to be a multiple-choice test, we must build it of good multiple-choice test items, not bad ones. The difference is critical. Quality performance assessments—that is, assessments that rely on observation and professional judgment—are made up of high-quality performance tasks and scoring guidelines only. So it is with essay assessments also. Each method brings with it a set of specific procedural guidelines for developing high-quality ingredients capable of yielding dependable results.

However, a proper method, an appropriate sample, and good items, while essential, do not, by themselves, guarantee quality. As it turns out, each method carries with it a list of things that can go wrong that can mislead us and our students about their achievement. They can have the effect of *biasing* results. For instance, problems can arise during the administration (such as distractions) and scoring (such as unclear scoring criteria leading to evaluator bias), for example, that can adversely impact scores. As a result, the developers of any assessment must understanding those potential sources of bias and know what to do by way of assessment development and implementation to prevent such problems.

In this chapter, I address these matters for each of the four assessment methods (selected response, written response or essay, performance assessment, and direct personal interaction with the student), suggesting sampling ideas and attributes of quality ingredients first and then outlining potential sources of bias for all at the end of the chapter. In addition, I offer a few simple suggestions for using each assessment method to support student learning.

SELECTED RESPONSE TEST DEVELOPMENT

This format includes multiple choice, true/false, matching and fill in items. The test development process for these kinds of tests includes these steps in this order:

1. Develop an assessment plan or blueprint that identifies an appropriate sample of achievement.
2. Identify the specific elements of knowledge and understanding or reasoning to be assessed.
3. Transform those elements into test items and answer key.

Sampling

Assessors face a two-part challenge here: make a sampling plan that covers the important material to be learned and then decide what specific elements of content will be the focus of the actual test items.

Make a Plan

Remember from the targets-by-methods match chapter that this method aligns well with content knowledge targets and with relatively simple patterns of reasoning. The power of selected response resides in its great efficiency in sampling these kinds of targets. Because each item requires a relatively brief response time, one can sample large domains with enough items or small domains with great depth. Further, these formats permit rapid optical scan scoring using technology that can yield digital reports of results in a variety of useful forms.

Realize, however, that it is only appropriate to use selected response formats when we are certain students have a sufficiently high level of reading proficiency to be able to comprehend the test items. This problem is rare at the post-secondary level, but it is not unheard of.

One very specific strategy for sampling planning for a selected response test is to build a test blueprint. This is a design plan for a test that works just like a blueprint for a house: make a plan and build the house we want. Make a test plan that reflects the learning priorities and we lay the foundation for a quality test. Figure 5.1 provides a simple example of such a blueprint.

Table 5.1
Sample Test Blueprint

Content	Knowledge & Understanding	Comparative Reasoning	Classification Reasoning	Total
Forms of Government	9 questions	5	1	15
Structure of US Government	4	5	1	10
Citizen Rights, Responsibilities	7	5	3	15
Total	20	15	5	40

Note that there are several categories of content to be sampled, each to be reflected in the total number of test items listed in the far right column—a reflection of the relative priorities where categories that the instructor thinks are more important get more items. Note also that, in the columns, priority patterns of reasoning are identified, again reflected in their relative emphasis in terms of the number of items assigned to each at the bottom of the column.

Just a quick reminder about reasoning targets: Remember in the Chapter 3 description of types of targets, the options began with content knowledge and understanding (a foundation of academic competence in all academic disciplines) and then went on to the expectation that students would learn to use that knowledge to reason and solve problems. Every academic discipline defines itself, at least in part, in terms of consistent patterns of reasoning to be mastered: algorithmic math problem solving processes, applications of the discipline of scientific inquiry, reading comprehensions, composing original text in writing, comparative reasoning, inferential reasoning, classification, analytical reasoning, evaluative reasoning, etc. As specified in Chapter 3, it is the responsibility of the faculty to define those reasoning proficiencies that are relevant for their students to master and to share those with their students from the very beginning of instruction.

Once the content knowledge and reasoning priorities have been established by the instructor for a particular test, then the sampling plan can be filled in by filtering the row and column totals up into the cells of the table so they add correctly to those totals. So in Figure 5-1, we find that we need to compose a certain number of questions for each cell of the blueprint to cover the domain of instructional and priorities. Here is why this is key to sound sampling:

Any test item asks students to do two things: dip into their memory to retrieve some element(s) of knowledge (if it is, indeed, there) and then carry out some cognitive operation using that knowledge to arrive at the right answer. So, for example, I need 5 items that require students to use their knowledge of Forms of Government to reason comparatively to get to the right answer—that is, to identify similarities or differences. Once the number of items is specified for each cell of the table, a portrait emerges of the number of items needed in each cell to sample row (content) and column (reasoning) priorities.

Please realize that it is completely possible that some learning contexts might center only on content knowledge priorities as students are gain the foundations they need for later use of their knowledge. In such cases, a one-column table would be all we would need. It is always the case that you set these priorities. Just make absolutely sure your students are given the opportunity to learn to hit all of the content and reasoning targets in the blueprint. No surprises and no excuses.

Selecting the Elements of Content to Be Tested

The next question is, what specific pieces of content should I test in each cell? This, once again, is a matter of the instructor's priorities. To determine this, start by *reviewing the body of material to be learned, identifying and writing down in complete sentence* form as you go the most important individual elements knowledge or reasoning you want students to know. Each sentence will for the foundation of a test item. This is a huge time saver step that enhances test quality immensely. By starting item in this way, one sharpens the focus of test items and, as it turns out, one makes test development much quicker and easier. Identify and write down the number of such important learnings needed for each cell of the test blueprint. In Figure 5-1, this means one would need 9 sentences for the first (top right) cell, 4 sentences for the next cell down, etc.

When all important learning sentences have been selected and written down, let the list rest for a while (day or so). Then return to it, reading through the sentences and asking of each, does this really reflect my instructional priorities? Then take a bigger perspective: Does the entire list sentences, considered together, really capture what I feel is important? Have I included trivial materials? Is anything that is really important missing? Adjust as needed by substituting new important learning where needed.

Remember the sampling goal: For any given body of material, one must collect enough important learnings to confidently generalize from that students' performance on the sample (score on the test) to their probable mastery of the whole. One cannot ask everything. But one needs to be sure to ask enough. It's a matter of professional judgment by the content expert and, as the test creator, you are that judge.

Item Writing

The sentences written and collected as above yield test items with almost no effort. Here's why:

- Simply place the sentence on a true/false test as a true item
- Make part wrong and include it as a false item
- Remove a key part of the sentence and turn it into a fill-in item
- Posit alternative responses to the fill-in, one of which is correct or best and create a multiple choice item

Clearly, then, the foundation of a good test item is the essential learning upon which it focuses. Every minute invested in the process of selecting and refining the essential learnings sentences saves time and improves quality.

As each test item takes shape, follow the specific item writing guidelines listed below to assure quality:

When developing multiple-choice test items, keep these few simple, yet powerful, guidelines in mind:

1. Write clearly. Good selected response assessment development is first and foremost an exercise in clear communication. Be brief and very clear.

2. Ask a question. When using multiple-choice and fill-in formats, pose a question to be answered; minimize the use of incomplete statements as item stems. Use this trigger for example:: "Which is the following is an attribute of a good test item?" Not this: "You can identify a good test item because it:" When you force yourself to ask a question, you force yourself to express a complete thought in the stem which usually promotes clear understanding.

3. Eliminate clues to the correct answer either within the question or across questions within a test. When grammatical clues within items or material presented in other items give away the correct answer, students get items right for the wrong reasons.

4. Don't repeat the same words within each response option; rather, reword the item stem to move the repetitive material up there. This will clarify the problem and make it more efficient for respondents to read.

5. Be sure there is only one correct or best answer. It is acceptable to ask respondents to select a best answer from among a set of answers, all of which are correct. Just be sure to word the question so as to make it clear that they are to find the "best answer."

6. *Word response options as briefly as possible and be sure they are grammatically parallel.* This has two desirable effects. First, it makes items easier to read. Second, it helps eliminate grammatical clues to the correct answer.

7. *Vary the number of response options presented as needed to pose the problem you want your students to solve.* While it is best to design multiple-choice questions around three, four, or five response options, it is permissible to vary the number of response options offered across items within the same test. Try not to use "all of the above" or "none of the above" merely to fill up spaces just because you can't think of other incorrect answers. Use them only when they fit the context of the question.

8. *Double-check the scoring key for accuracy before scoring.* Enough said.

By the way, here's a simple, yet very effective, multiple-choice test item writing tip: If you compose a multiple-choice item and find that you cannot think of enough plausible incorrect responses, include the item on a test the first time as a fill-in question. As your students respond, those who get it wrong will provide you with the full range of viable incorrect responses you need the next time you use it.

Guidelines for True/False Exercises

Just one simple guideline here: Regardless of the content being tested, make the item *entirely* true or entirely false *as stated*. Complex "idea salads" including some truth and some falsehood just confuse the issue. Precisely what is the idea you're testing? State it and move on to the next one.

Guidelines for Matching Items

When developing matching exercises, follow all of the multiple-choice guidelines offered previously. In addition, observe the following guidelines:

1. Provide clear and concise directions for making the match.

2. Keep the list of things to be matched short. The maximum number of options is 10. Shorter is better.

3. Keep the list of things to be matched homogeneous. Don't mix events with dates or with names, etc. Again, idea salads confuse the focus.

5. Keep the list of response options brief in their wording and parallel in construction. Pose the matching challenge in clear, straightforward language.

6. Include more response options than stems and permit students to use response options more than once. This has the effect of making it impossible for students to arrive at the correct response purely through a process of elimination.

Guidelines for Fill-in Items

Here there are two simple guidelines to follow:

1. Ask respondents a question and provide space for an answer. This forces you to express a complete thought. The use of incomplete statements as item stems is acceptable. But if you use them, be sure to capture the essence of the problem in that stem.

2. Try to stick to one blank per item. Come to the point. Ask one question, get one answer, and move on. Use only simple language, complete communication, clear conclusions. Does the student know the answer or not?

Using Assessment to Support Learning

Here are some ways to use the classroom assessment process while students are still learning to enhance their learning:

- Share the blueprint for a unit final exam with students on the first day of the unit.
- Engage students as partners in the process of identifying key essential learning sentences—with your help, they can begin to zero in on your priorities
- Ask them to write practice items like those they think might appear on the final exam and have them practice answering each other's questions, defending their answers
- Create a parallel form of the unit final (different items but same priorities) and use it as a pretest; engage students as partners in analyzing results by row and column of the blueprint to see their beginning point
- Use the practice test two days before the official final and help students see where to focus their final preparation.

DEVELOPING ESSAY ASSESSMENTS

Designing and developing these assessments involves three steps:

1. Development of an assessment plan or blueprint to sample learning

2. Exercise development
3. Development of scoring guides

Test planning for this form of assessment is very much like planning selected response assessments. While exercise development is a bit easier, scoring preparation is much more challenging.

Sampling

On the whole, essay assessment offers great flexibility. It can provide useful information on student mastery of larger structures of knowledge where relationships among elements are important, reasoning and problem-solving proficiencies, and mastery of procedural knowledge prerequisite to performance skills or product development. But to tap these learning targets successfully, one must invest thoughtful preparation time in writing exercises that challenge respondents by describing a complete and novel task.

A blueprint for an essay assessment can look very much like a plan for a selected response tests. However, rather than entering the number of items for each row, column, and cell according to content priorities, one enters the number of points to be distributed across the plan. Essay exercises and scoring guides, each of which counts for a pre-specified number of points, are then developed to satisfy those sampling requirements.

Blueprints for assessments that combine selected response and essay formats also identify the number of points assigned to each row, column and cell of the table of specifications. Then points are distributed among items at the rate of one point for selected response items and among essay exercises as appropriate for each resulting in the totals of the blueprint.

In order to sample in a manner that leads to confident generalizations about student learning, don't offer students choices regarding the exercises to which they can respond. The assessment question should always be, "Can you hit the agreed-on target?" It should never be, "Can you hit the target if you get to define it?", or "Which part of the agreed-on target are you most confident that you can hit?" These latter questions always leave the assessor uncertain about whether students have in fact mastered the material covered in exercises not selected, some of which may be crucial to later learning. When students select their own sample of performance, it can be a biased one.

Here is one final sampling idea: Let's say one wishes to assess students' reasoning proficiencies but in a domain where you do *not* expect your students to know the content outright or you are not sure all students have a sufficient or equal grasp of the underlying body of knowledge. You can use what we call an "interpretive exercise." Simply provide a chart, graph, table, or paragraph presenting the knowledge to be used and accompany it with a set of test question or essay exercises requiring the use of the material presented.

Exercise Development

Sound essay exercises accomplish three things:

1. Specify the knowledge students are supposed to bring to bear in preparing a response.
2. Specify the kind(s) of reasoning or problem solving respondents are to carry out. Be clear about what respondents are to write about.
3. Point the direction to an appropriate response without giving away the answer.

In other words, good exercises literally list the key elements of a good response without cueing the unprepared examinee on how to succeed.

One excellent way to check the quality of your essay exercises is to try to write or outline a high-quality response yourself. If you can, you probably have a properly focused exercise. If you cannot, it needs work. Besides, this process will serve you well in your next step, devising scoring criteria.

In preparing for such an assessment, be clear with students that it is the content of their answer that counts rather than its form. Then make sure you score responses accordingly—more about that below. But for now suffice it to say that it should be the quality of the ideas and reasoning that counts. Urge them to communicate their understanding and problem solutions as efficiently as they can by relying on outlines and lists of ideas, examples, illustrations, charts, whatever it takes to come to the point quickly and clearly. This speeds scoring immensely.

Developing Essay Scoring Procedures

Many educators score written responses by applying what could be called "floating standards," in which one waits to see what responses one gets to decide what one wanted. This represents the ultimate in unsound assessment practice because it destroys both the validity and reliability of the assessment.

In that regard, adhere to the instructional and assessment philosophy that has guided everything discussed up to this point: Students are more likely to succeed if they know what success looks like from the beginning of the learning. State the meaning of success up front, design instruction to help students succeed, and devise and use assessments that reflect that vision of success. That includes formulating essay scoring criteria in advance and holding yourself and your students accountable for attaining those standards.

When a student writes an essay, it is possible to judge three different qualities of that work. We can evaluate whether the student's work conveys any or all of the following:

- Accurate knowledge and understanding
- Proper use of that knowledge in a manner that represents sound reasoning
- Effective written communication

The first two focus on matters of substance or content of the essay, while the latter centers on matters of form. In the context of essay assessment, it is most appropriate to the substance or content of essays: accuracy of knowledge and quality of reasoning. When one centers on the quality of the writing, the format changes to performance assessment. A rubric for evaluating the writing quality will be provided in the next section on that format. But understand that this would only be appropriate in context where one is teaching and evaluating keys to effective writing.

Essay Scoring Options

Typically, we convey evaluative judgments about essay quality in terms of the number of points attained by the student. There are two acceptable ways to do this, with the checklist and scoring rubrics. Please note that scoring guides in essay assessment are exercise-specific. That is, you create a separate and specific scoring guide for each new exercise, being sure to focus on keys to success in that specific context. One way to do this is by developing and applying a checklist of key ingredients expected in a quality answer. Award points when specific ingredients appear in students' answers. In this case, the scoring guide calls for respondents to cover certain material. They receive points for each key point they cover.

A second option is to define achievement in terms of one or more performance continua. For example, a three-point rating scale might define three levels of mastery of the required material and we would apply that scale to each student's response. Here's an example:

3   The response is clear, focused, and accurate. Relevant points are made (in terms of the content expectations or kinds of reasoning sought by the exercise) with good support (derived from the content to be used, again as spelled out in the exercise). Good connections are drawn and important insights are evident.
2   The answer is clear and somewhat focused, but not compelling. Support of points made is limited. Connections are fuzzy, leading to few insights.
1   The response misses the point, contains inaccurate information, or otherwise demonstrates lack of mastery of the material. Points are unclear, support is missing, and/or no insights are included.

Some teachers devise such scoring rubrics to apply in a "holistic" manner, like this example. In this case, one overall judgment captures the teacher's evaluation of the essay. Other times teachers devise multiple "analytical" scales for the same essay, permitting them to evaluate the content coverage of the response separately from other important features. The idea is to develop as many such scales as needed to evaluate the particular material you are rating. Criteria for ratings, for example, might include these factors:

70

- Demonstrated mastery of content
- Organization of ideas
- Soundness of the reasoning demonstrated

Whether using holistic or analytical rubrics, however, the more specific and focused the criteria, the more dependable will be the results.

Using Assessment to Support Learning

As with selected response methods, during their learning, the more students can come to understand about the valued learning targets, the more they are likely to learn and the more confident they are likely to become as learners. Share the assessment blueprint from the very beginning of a unit of study. Engage students in drafting essay exercises along with their own scoring schemes. Use these during instruction to refine their sense of the meaning of success and to help them develop key understandings. Have students practice responding to each other's essays and scoring each other's responses.

DEVELOPING PERFORMANCE ASSESSMENTS

College-level learning experiences often include circumstances where students must perform in certain ways so that an evaluator can observe and make judgments about the quality of their performance. Such performances are observed and evaluated in English and foreign language speech, the arts, science laboratory contexts, and the like. Instructors observe and evaluate products created by their students—term papers, research or lab reports, visual or sculptural arts, etc. In each case, the key to evaluator success is to have formulated clear and appropriate criteria to defend a judgment of quality. This is the practice of performance assessment.

As with essay assessments, the goal is to make these subjective judgments as objective (free of bias) as they can be. We accomplish this by devising and learning to apply clear and appropriate performance criteria and gathering enough evidence (including enough performance tasks to sample adequately).

Because of the subjective nature of performance assessment, you, the rater, become potential source of bias. If the performance criteria you apply in evaluating student work are incorrect, imprecise, or influenced by factors unrelated to the student's actual achievement (such as gender, prior performance, etc.), the filters through which you see and evaluate that work can lead you to inaccurate judgments about proficiency.

To prevent such occurrences, establish sound performance criteria and learn to apply them consistently. The gauge of consistency that we apply in such assessment contexts is that of *inter-rater agreement*. Performance criteria are being applied consistently when two raters evaluate the same piece of work using the same criteria and, without conversing about it, draw the same conclusion about the level of proficiency demonstrated in that work. Surely you can see that, if they disagree, the judgment of student proficiency would be a function of who does the judging versus actual level of achievement. That would be unfair. So our goal always is to be so clear about the attributes of good performance and so crisp and clean in our description of levels of proficiency in the performance continuum that consistency in judgment would always be within reach.

Sampling

Performance assessment can provide dependable information about student achievement of some, but not all, kinds of valued targets. As we have established, if the objective is to assess student mastery content knowledge, observing and judging complex performance or products may not be the best way to find out if they have learned the material. It's not that you can't assess knowledge and understanding with this method. But problems can arise. Assume, for example, that you ask students to participate in a group discussion in Spanish so you can assess their mastery of Spanish fluency. Although this is an apparently authentic performance assessment, it might lead you to incorrect conclusions about students' language mastery. They will choose to use only vocabulary and syntax with which they are most comfortable and confident, avoiding vocabulary and constructions unfamiliar to them. Thus, you will see a biased sample of their content mastery. So when assessing student mastery of content knowledge, whether learned outright or retrieved through the use of references, selected response or essay formats are usually better choices.

Performance assessment can provide a means of assessing student reasoning and problem-solving proficiency. For example, one might give chemistry students unidentified substances to identify and watch how they go about setting up the apparatus and carrying out the study. The performance criteria would have to reflect the proper order of activities for conducting such experiments—an example of analytical reasoning. Those who reason well will follow the proper sequence and succeed. In this case, the process is as important as getting the right answer—the process is what is being assessed.

One also can use performance assessment to evaluated skills beyond those of proper reasoning. The great strength of this methodology lies in its ability to provide a dependable means of evaluating skills as they are doing the things that reflect certain forms of achievement, such as in artistic performance, technical or industrial proficiency, physical education, and oral proficiency in speaking a foreign language.

There are occasions when instructors ask students to create complex achievement-related products. The quality of those products indicates the creator's level of achievement. If we develop sound performance criteria that reflect the key attributes of these products and learn to apply those criteria well, performance assessment can serve us as both an efficient and effective tool.

The overarching sampling challenge in this context is best characterized by the question, how many performance task responses do you need to evaluate to judge proficiency? As in all classroom assessment situations, the answer is a matter of the professional judgment of the assessor. There are no rigid rules. But the art of making this judgment can be informed by these kinds of considerations:

- If a student's response to one task yields a great deal of evidence, then not many will be needed
- The higher the stakes of the decision that hangs in the balance (the more important the decision), then surer the judge of proficiency must be and the more evidence should be gathered
- The simpler the learning target (criteria) the fewer examples might be needed; the more complex the learning target, the more evidence might be needed

Based on these considerations, it becomes clear that the starting place for the creation of a high-quality performance assessment is the articulation of the performance to be evaluated.

Defining Success: Scoring Guides

This design decision asks us to answer these basic questions: How will successful achievement manifest itself? Where will we most easily find evidence of proficiency? And, will it take the form of a particular set of performance skills—behaviors that students must demonstrate? Or, will we observe and judge something students have created (a product) in order to determine their proficiency? Note also, that some performance assessments might focus both on skills and products that result, such as when we assess the computer programming process and then the quality of the resulting program

The scoring guide is the part of the performance assessment design where we describe what "counts." The challenge is to not only describe what "outstanding" performance looks like, but also to map each of the different levels of performance starting with poor quality and leading up to the highest quality. We strive to do this with descriptive language. So in this sense, rubrics provide the vocabulary we need to communicate with our students about the path to successful performance.

In one sense, accomplished faculty members are connoisseurs of good performance, but in another sense, they must be far more than that. Connoisseurs can recognize and appreciate outstanding performance when they see it. They can describe why they believe something is outstanding or not.

Faculty members must be very much like these connoisseurs in that they too must be able to recognize and describe outstanding performance. But for accomplished teachers, there is much more. Not only can well-prepared teachers visualize and explain the meaning of success, but they also can impart that meaning to others so as to help them become outstanding performers. *In short, they don't just criticize—they inspire and can promote improvement.*

To develop one's own scoring guides or rubrics, one must carry out a thoughtful task analysis of the performance skill or product to be evaluated. That means look inside the skills or products of interest to find the active ingredients. In most cases, this is not complicated. It can be done in a series of steps. To complete them successfully, one must have access to samples of student work that vary in quality from outstanding to very poor quality.

In fact, consider using these samples in collaboration with your students to devise scoring rubrics. Their involvement in this process can set them up for very high levels of learning success:

Step 1: Discover. The goal in this initial step is to help students begin to discover the keys to their own success. This requires that they become partners in the task or product analysis that will identify the active ingredients contributing to different levels of proficiency. As their teacher, you engage students in answering the question, how does a good task or product differ from a poor-quality one? To do this, students must have the opportunity to see, study and discuss the examples. Engage them in the process of brainstorming as many differences as they can find. You will notice right away the power of asking students to contrast examples of vastly different samples of performance. It virtually always helps them zero in on how to describe performance, good and poor, in their own clear and understandable language.

Step 2: Condensing. Next help students build a vocabulary that both you and they can use to converse with each other about performance. This is why it is important to engage students in learning the rubric. Do this by engaging them in the process of organizing, outlining or subsuming the Step 1 brainstormed list into a smaller more manageable number of key differentiating ingredients. When you share the stage with your students and involve them in defining success by having them analyze examples and choose the language to describe achievement, in effect you begin to connect them to their target.

Step 3: Defining. In this step, it is crucial to remember that the job is not merely to define successful, or high-level, performance. Rather, one seeks to describe the full range of performance, so each performer can come to understand at any point in time where they are now in relation to where we want them to be down the road. Only with that road map in hand can they watch themselves travel their own personal journey to excellence, feeling in complete control all along the way.

Accomplish this by collaborating with students in the development of a performance or quality continuum—a rating scale—for each key ingredient. What does outstanding work look like for that ingredient? Use descriptive language. What does very poor quality look like—again, describe it. What does mid-range quality look like? See Table 5.2 for an example. I will say much more about this below.

Step 4: Learn to Apply the Rubric. The next step is to help your students learn to apply their performance criteria through practice. You accomplish this most effectively by providing them with more examples of performance that vary greatly in quality so they can analyze and judge quality. As this process unfolds, you can start your students down the road of discovering their own current level of performance using agreed-on rubrics. (When your students become trained raters, the scoring work load spreads over many shoulders.) With this practice completed, have them produce some of their own work and evaluate it for quality, In this way, you show them where they are now in relation to where you want them to be, so they can begin to take charge of their journey to excellence.

Step 5: Refining. The process of revising and refining scoring rubrics never stops. By evaluating lots of student work over time, one tunes into the keys to success with increasing focus and precision. As new insights arise, revise your criteria to reflect your best current thinking. And remember, it is not uncommon for students who are involved in the process to "out think" their instructors and come up with dimensions of excellence that you have not seen. When they do, honor their good thinking! Never regard performance criteria as "finished." Rather, always see them as works in progress.

And remember, when students are partners in carrying out these steps, you and they join together to become a learning community. Together, you open windows to the meaning of academic success, providing your students with the words and examples they need to see and to achieve that vision.

The Attributes of Good Scoring Guides

Complete scoring guides for evaluating student proficiency in a performance assessment context specify the *important content* (what counts in a student's work) with sharp *clarity* (everyone understands what is meant by quality).

Scoring guides rate high in *content coverage* when everything of importance is included—nothing of importance is left out. But they do leave out things that are regarded as unimportant—tangential to student success. Here are some questions to ask to evaluate the appropriateness of a rubric's content:

- Does the content included represent the best current thinking of the field regarding keys to successful performance?
- Does the content align with relevant state or district achievement standards?
- Does the content have the "ring of truth," or is it consistent with what you really look for in evaluating student work?

- Are the criteria divided into well organized and understandable pieces?
- Can you distinguish clearly among the levels of performance defined in the rubric?

They rate high when the are well *organized* and *clear*—when it's easy for everyone involved (student and teacher alike) to understand what is meant. Terms are defined, as is each level of proficiency. Samples of student work have been collected to illustrate the various levels of performance.

Figure 5.2 provides quality rating scales for each of the attributes of a good scoring guide described below. Collections of scoring criteria arrayed in this manner are often referred to in the professional literature as "rubrics".

Devising Performance Tasks

Performance assessment tasks, like selected response test items and essay exercises, frame the assignment for students. Thus, performance assessment tasks clearly and explicitly elicit evidence of the respondent's level of mastery of the intended achievement target(s). Two basic design considerations must be addressed:

- The specific ingredients of the task, defining what performers are to do
- The number of tasks needed to sample performance

Like well-developed essay exercises, sound performance assessment tasks specify and explain the challenge to respondents, while setting them up to succeed if they can, by doing the following:

- Identify the specific kind(s) of performance to be demonstrated
- Detail the context and conditions within which proficiency will be demonstrated
- Remind respondents of the scoring criteria to be applied

Quality tasks address the right *content*. They elicit the correct response—a performance that reveals the proper proficiency. In other words it is obvious that the response can be effectively evaluated using the scoring criteria or rubric. The two align. When the achievement target is simple in its nature, the task reflects that simplicity: to assess oral reading fluency, have students read. When the target is more complex, so is the task: to assess proficiency in preparing a science research paper, create the paper.

And finally, quality tasks provide specific in their instructions to the student. There is no confusing in the mind of the student—each student knows exactly what to do. Quality tasks are feasible for use in the classroom. It is practical given the realities of the context. Students have enough time to respond. Proper materials and equipment are readily available for all respondents. Time is available to examine and evaluate performance using the previously developed scoring criteria. In short, there is nothing about the task set in its context that will give rise to an inaccurate picture of the student's proficiency.

In Figure 5.3 below, you will find a set of rating scales or rubrics you can used to judge the quality of your performance tasks.

Table 5.2

Developing High-quality Performance Assessment Scoring Guides

Content: What does the rubric assess?

Indicator	Level 3: Ready to Use	Level 2: Needs Some Revision	Level 1: Completely Revise or Don't Use
Target Alignment	Criteria and descriptors align directly with the content standards or learning targets they are intended to assess.	The rubric includes one or two small features that are not related to the intended content standards or learning targets	The rubric focuses on features that are not related to the intended content standards or learning targets. One or more of the following applies: • The criteria and descriptors inappropriately focus on dimensions of the task rather than the learning targets. • The learning targets are not clear.
Match to Essential Elements	Criteria and descriptors represent best thinking in the field about what it means to perform well on the content standards or learning targets. • Everything of importance (for students at your level) has been included. Trivial and unrelated features are left out.	A few descriptors might be irrelevant or unimportant for defining proficiency, but most are relevant.	You can think of many important indicators of quality that are missing, the rubric focuses on irrelevant features, or you find yourself asking, "Why should students have to do it *this* way?"

81

Organization: Are the scoring criteria organized logically?

Indicator	Level 3: Ready to Use	Level 2: Needs Some Revision	Level 1: Completely Revise or Don't Use
Number of Criteria	The number of criteria reflects the complexity of the learning target and its intended use • If the rubric is holistic, a single scale sufficiently represents the target or the use is solely summative. • If the target is complex and the use is formative, the rubric is analytic; the number of criteria appropriately define categories of proficiency.	If a rubric is analytic, the number of criteria needs to be adjusted: either a single criterion should be made into two or more criteria, or two or more criteria should be combined.	The rubric is holistic (a single scale) when it needs to be analytic (multiple criteria) to better reflect the level of complexity of the learning targets to be assessed and the intended use of the data.
Independence of Criteria	If there are multiple criteria, they are independent of one another—the same or similar features are represented in only one of the criterion.	The criteria are mostly independent of one another, but in some cases features are represented in more than one criterion.	The criteria are not independent of one another. The same or similar features are represented in multiple criteria throughout the rubric, to the extent that the criteria do not function as separate categories.
Grouping of Descriptors	If there are multiple criteria, indicators and descriptors are grouped logically within each criterion. All descriptors fit under the criterion in which they are placed.	Most indicators and descriptors under a criterion are placed correctly, but a few need to be moved to a different criterion.	Indicators and descriptors that go together don't seem to be placed together; descriptors that are different are placed together; the categories don't work.

Number of Levels	The number of levels fits complexity of the target and intended use of the results. There are enough levels to reflect typical stages of student understanding, capabilities, or progress, but not so many that it is impossible to distinguish among them.	There are a few too many levels of quality to distinguish among, so some will need to be merged, or, there are not quite enough levels to reflect typical stages of student growth, so more will have to be created.	The number of levels is inappropriate for the learning target being assessed or the intended use of the rubric. One or more of the following is true • There are so many levels it is impossible to reliably distinguish among them • There are far too few levels to be useful in tracking student growth. • It is impossible to define the number of levels indicated.

Clarity: Are the details clearly spelled out?

Indicator	Level 3: Ready to Use	Level 2: Needs Some Revision	Level 1: Completely Revise or Don't Use
Kind of Detail	Wording is descriptive of the work to be performed. There is enough detail that it is possible to match a student performance or product to the appropriate level. Descriptors provide an accurate explanation of the characteristics of quality. If counting the number or frequency of something is included as an indicator, changes in such counts *are* indicators of changes in quality.	Wording is mostly descriptive, but has one or more problems: • The rubric includes a few terms that are vague. • Some language is evaluative rather than descriptive of the work. • Only the top level of quality is described sufficiently; the other levels include insufficient or no descriptive detail. • The rubric mostly avoids frequency counts, but there are a few times that counts are used even though changes in such counts do not equate to changes in level of quality.	Wording is not clear. One or more problems exist: Descriptors consist of vague terms without clarification, e.g., "extremely," "thoroughly," "completely," or "insightful." • Descriptors rely heavily on evaluative language to differentiate levels of quality, e.g., "mediocre," "clever," or "above average." • The rubric is little more than a list of categories and a rating scale. • Descriptors consist almost solely of counting the number or frequency of something, when quantity does not equate to quality.

Indicator	Level 3: Ready to Use	Level 2: Needs Some Revision	Level 1: Completely Revise or Don't Use
Content of Levels	The features described across the levels are parallel in content. If a feature is present in one level, it is present in all levels. If a feature is missing at one or more levels, there is a logical rationale.	The levels of the rubric are mostly parallel in content. One or a few descriptors of quality at one level are missing at other levels when they should be present.	The levels of the rubric are not parallel in content. Most descriptors of quality are not represented at all levels and there is not an adequate rationale for their omission.
Formative Usefulness	If the rubric is intended for use in supporting learning, its language can be effective feedback to the student and the teacher, describing strengths and areas needing work in sufficient detail to guide further learning. • Students can easily use the rubric to revise their own work • Teachers can translate results into instruction	If the rubric is intended for formative use, some parts can function as effective feedback to the student and the teacher, describing strengths and areas needing work in sufficient detail to guide planning for further learning. Descriptors in other parts need refining to accomplish this purpose.	If the rubric is intended for formative use, it cannot be used provide effective feedback to students and teachers because it doesn't describe strengths and areas needing work in sufficient detail to guide next steps in learning.

Table 5.3
Rubric for Tasks

Content: What learning will the task demonstrate?

Indicator	Level 3: Ready to Use	Level 2: Needs Some Revision	Level 1: Completely Revise or Don't Use
Target Alignment	All requirements of the task are directly aligned to the learning target(s) to be assessed. The task will elicit a performance that could be used to judge proficiency on the intended learning targets.	Some requirements of the task are not aligned to the learning target(s) to be assessed. There is extra work in this task not needed to assess the intended learning targets.	Requirements of the task are not aligned to the learning target(s) to be assessed. The task will not elicit a performance that could be used to judge proficiency on the intended learning targets.
Authenticity	The task provides as realistic a context as possible, given the learning target and intended use of the information. The conditions model application of the learning to a practical situation found in life beyond school.	The task provides an artificial context. The conditions do not provide a clear link to application of the learning to situations found in life beyond school.	The task either provides no context, when it would be appropriate to provide one, or the context does not lead students to see how the learning could apply to situations found in life beyond school.
Choice	If the task allows students to choose different tasks, it is clear that all choices will provide evidence of achievement on the same learning targets. All choices ask for the same performance or product, with approximately the same level of difficulty, and under the same conditions.	If the task allows students to choose different tasks, some of the choices may relate to different learning targets, or there is some variation in performance or product called for, level of difficulty, or conditions.	If the task allows students to choose different tasks, none of the choices relate to the same learning target, or there is considerable variation in performance or product called for, level of difficulty, and/or conditions.

Indicator	Level 3: Ready to Use	Level 2: Needs Some Revision	Level 1: Completely Revise or Don't Use
Interference	Successful completion of the task does not depend on skills unrelated to the target being measured (e.g., intensive reading in a mathematics task). The task is culturally robust. Successful completion is not dependent on having had one particular cultural or linguistic background.	Successful completion of the task may be slightly influenced by skills unrelated to the target being measured. Successful completion of the task may be slightly influenced by having had one particular cultural or linguistic background.	Successful completion of the task depends on skills unrelated to the target being measured (e.g., intensive reading in a mathematics task). The task is not culturally robust. Successful completion depends on having had one particular cultural or linguistic background.
Resources	All resources required to complete the task successfully are available to all students.	Some students may have difficulty obtaining the necessary resources to complete the task successfully, or one or more of the resources required will be difficult for most students to obtain.	Many or most students will have difficulty accessing the resources necessary to complete the task successfully.

Information Provided: Are the directions and guidance given clear and sufficient?

Indicator	Level 3: Ready to Use	Level 2: Needs Some Revision	Level 1: Completely Revise or Don't Use
Instructions	The instructions are clear and unambiguous.	The instructions may leave room for erroneous interpretation of what is expected.	The instructions are confusing and frustrating to students.
Supplemental Information	The task includes the following information: • The knowledge students are to use in creating the task • The performance or product students are to create—what form it should take • The materials to be used, if any • Timeline for completion	Some of the following information is clear; some is unclear or missing: • The knowledge students are to use in creating the task • The performance or product students are to create—what form it should take • The materials to be used, if any • Timeline for completion	The task does not include the following information: • The knowledge students are to use in creating the task • The performance or product students are to create—what form it should take • The materials to be used, if any • Timeline for completion
Time Allowed	The time allowed for the task is sufficient for successful completion.	The time allowed is too long or too short, but either the timeline or the task can be adjusted.	The task will considerably more time than is allowed and cannot be broken into shorter segments.

Indicator	Level 3: Ready to Use	Level 2: Needs Some Revision	Level 1: Completely Revise or Don't Use
Level of Scaffolding	The task information is sufficient to let students know what they are to do without giving so much information that the task will no longer measure level of mastery of the intended learning target. The content points the way to success without doing the thinking for the student.	Some parts of the task may give students too much help. In some places, the task does the thinking or the work for the student, compromising the results or the learning.	The task is over-scaffolded. If used for summative purposes, the task cannot measure students' ability to create the product or performance independently, because the content is so explicit that students can follow it like a recipe. If used formatively, students can satisfactorily complete the task without having learned anything. The task measures only students' ability to follow directions.
Conditions	If a task assesses a performance skill, it specifies the conditions under which the performance or demonstration is to take place.	If a task assesses a performance skill, it does not sufficiently specify the conditions under which the performance or demonstration is to take place.	If a task assesses a performance skill, it does not give any indication of the conditions under which the performance or demonstration is to take place.
Help Allowed	Multi-day tasks specify the help allowed.	Although there is some reference to what kind of help is allowed for multi-day tasks, it could be misinterpreted.	Multi-day tasks do not specify the help allowed.
Criteria	The task includes a description of (or reference to) the criteria by which the performance or product will be judged. Students are familiar with the criteria.	Although described or referred to, the criteria by which the performance or product will be judged are vague or unclear (see *Rubric for Rubrics*).	The task includes no reference to the criteria by which the performance or product will be judged. or The students are not familiar with the criteria to be used.

Sampling—Is there enough evidence?

Indicator	Level 3: Ready to Use	Level 2: Needs Some Revision	Level 1: Completely Revise or Don't Use
Use of Information	The breadth of the task or the number of tasks or repeated instances of performance is sufficient to support the intended use of the information.	The task is broader than needed to support the intended use of the information. There are more tasks or repeated instances of performance than are needed to support the intended use of the information.	The breadth of the task or the number of tasks or repeated instances of performance is not sufficient support the intended use of the information.
Coverage of Target	The breadth of the task or the number of tasks or repeated instances of performance is sufficient to cover the breadth of the intended learning target.	The task is broader than needed to cover the breadth of the intended learning target. There are more tasks or repeated instances of performance than are needed to cover the breadth of the intended learning target.	The breadth of the task or the number of tasks or repeated instances of performance is not sufficient to cover the breadth of the intended learning target.

PERSONAL COMMUNICATION

Person to person interaction can provide instructors with keen insight into student learning. This kind of communication traditionally has formed the basis for oral examinations. Guidelines for this approach to assessment follow. Then we turn to other kinds of personal interaction that can support learning.

Oral Examinations

In this case, teachers create a sampling plan, devise questions, and then pose them to their students, who reflect and provide oral versus written responses. Teachers listen to and interpret those responses, evaluating quality and inferring levels of achievement. In a very real sense, this is like essay assessment, but with the added benefit of being able to ask follow-up questions.

While the oral examination tradition lost favor in the United States with the advent of selected response assessment during the last century, it still has great potential for use today, especially given the increasing complexity of our valued educational targets and the complexity and cost of setting up higher-fidelity performance assessments.

You can take advantage of the strengths of this format by adhering to some simple keys to its successful use:

- Develop brief exercises that focus on the desired targets(s).
- Rely on exercises that identify the knowledge to be brought to bear, specify the kind of reasoning students are to use, and identify the standards you will apply in evaluating responses.

- Develop written scoring criteria in advance of the assessment (refer back to the guidelines for developing scoring schemes for essay assessments provided earlier in this chapter).
- Be sure criteria separate content and reasoning targets from facility with verbal expression.
- Prepare in advance to accommodate the needs of any students who may confront language proficiency barriers.
- Have a checklist, rating scale, or other method of recording results ready to use at the time of the assessment.
- If necessary, record responses for later evaluation or reconsideration

Assessment Approaches that Can Support Learning

Even as teaching and learning is progressing (that is, during instruction), a few strategically placed questions can help you to monitor and adjust. But even beyond this, personal communication affords you some special opportunities. For example, unlike some other forms of assessment, if you are startled, puzzled, or pleased by a student's response, you can ask follow-up questions to dig more deeply to reveal student thinking. In other words, you can get beyond a particular response to explore its origins. If you find misconceptions, you can take immediate action to correct them.

If we vary that theme just a bit, we come upon another power of personal communication. You can attach those follow-up questions to any other mode of assessment to gain deeper understanding of student achievement. For instance, let's say a student fails a performance assessment and you wish to discover why in order to help that student find success next time (that is, assessment FOR learning). You can follow up the

91

failure with a few carefully phrased questions to see if it was due to a lack of prerequisite knowledge or to poor-quality reasoning on the student's part.

To the attentive user, students' nonverbal reactions can provide valuable insights into achievement and feelings about the material learned (or not learned). These indicators of confidence or uncertainty, excitement or boredom, and comfort or anxiety can lead you to probe more deeply into the underlying causes. With experience, good teachers begin to tune into students' facial expressions, posture, and spontaneous verbalizations as evidence in this case. This kind of perception checking can result in levels of student–teacher communication not achievable through the other assessment means. Consider the following options:

Instructional Questions and Answers

This has been a foundation of education since before Socrates. As instruction proceeds, the teacher poses questions for students to answer. This activity promotes thinking and learning, and also provides information about achievement. The teacher listens to answers, interprets them in terms of internally held standards, infers the respondent's level of attainment, and proceeds accordingly.

The following keys to successful use will help you take advantage of the strengths of this as an assessment format, while overcoming weaknesses:

• Plan key questions in advance of instruction, so as to ensure proper alignment with the target and with students' capabilities.

- Ask clear, brief questions that help students focus on a relatively narrow range of acceptable responses.
- Probe various kinds of reasoning, as appropriate.
- Ask the question first and then call on the person who is to respond. This will have the effect of keeping all students on focus.
- Call on both volunteer and non-volunteer respondents. This, too, will keep all students in the game.
- Acknowledge correct or high-quality responses; probe incorrect responses for underlying reasons.
- After posing a question, wait for a response. Let respondents know that you always expect a response and will wait for as long as it takes.

If the objective is to determine what our students know and understand, direct questioning of content will suffice. But if we want to help our students become active strategic reasoners, using their new insights to make meaning, the questions we pose for them are crucial to their success.

Questions need not always flow from teacher to student. Students can ask themselves key questions and then discuss their answers with you, their teacher.

Conferences and Interviews

Some student-instructor conferences serve as structured or unstructured audits of student achievement, in which the objective is to talk about what students have learned and have yet to learn. Participants talk directly and openly about levels of student attainment; comfort with the material the students are mastering; specific needs, interests, and desires; and/or any other achievement-related topics that contribute to an effective teaching and learning environment. In effect, teachers and students speak together in the service of understanding how to work effectively together.

Remember, interviews or conferences need not be conceived as every-pupil, standardized affairs, with each event a carbon copy of the others. You might meet with only one student, if it fills a communication need. Also, interviews or conferences might well vary in their focus with students who have different needs. The following are keys to your successful use of conference and interview assessment formats:

- Carefully think out and plan your questions in advance. Remember, students can share in their preparation.
- Plan for enough uninterrupted time to conduct the entire interview or conference.
- Be sure to conclude each meeting with a summary of the lessons learned and their implications for how you and the student will work together in the future.

One important strength of the interview or conference as a mode of assessment lies in the impact it can have on your student–instructor relationships. When conducted in a context where you have been up front about expectations, students understand the achievement target, and all involved are invested in student success, conferences have the effect of empowering students to take responsibility for at least part of the assessment of their own progress. Conducted in a context where everyone is committed to success and where academic success is clearly and openly defined, interviews inform and motivate both you and your students.

One can encourage students to lead these meetings. Have them plan questions they way to ask you in order to advance their learning. Or ask them to plan to share some of their work with you that reveals where they are now in relation to where they want to be so you can collaborate in planning what comes next in their learning.

Class Discussions

When students participate in class discussions, the things they say reveal a great deal about their achievements and their feelings. Discussions are instructor- or student-led group interactions in which the material to be mastered is explored from various perspectives. Instructors listen to the interaction, evaluate the quality of student contributions, and infer individual student or group achievement. Clearly, class discussions have the simultaneous effect of promoting both student learning and their ability to use what they know.

To take advantage of the strengths of this method of assessment, while minimizing the impact of potential weaknesses, follow these keys to successful use:

- Prepare questions or discussion issues in advance to focus sharply on the intended achievement target.
- Be sure students are aware of your focus in evaluating their contributions. Are you judging the content of students' contributions or the form of their contribution—how they communicate. Be clear about what it means to be good at each.
- Remember, the public display of achievement or lack thereof is risky in the eyes of some students. Provide those students with other more private means of demonstrating achievement.
- Contexts where achievement information derived from participation in discussion is to influence high-stakes decisions

(e.g., grading) keep dependable records of performance. Rely on more than you memory of their involvement.

THE MATTER OF ASSESSMENT BIAS

By way of brief summary, I have stipulated that they keys to good test development are beginning with a clear target, selecting a proper method and building the test out of sound exercises and scoring procedures. But in Chapter 1 I added a forth ingredient to good (accurate) assessment: minimizing bias that can distort test results and lead to the misrepresentation of achievement. By this I mean allowing factors other than the student's achievement to influence their test results. Outlined below is an array of some of the factors that can become barriers to accurate assessment. By and large, these potential problems can be avoided by following the guidelines for development high-quality assessments identified in the foregoing presentation.

Some of the most important sources of potential bias are these:

1. Sources common to all assessment methods:
   A. Potential barriers that can arise from *within the student*:
      * Language barriers keep them from understanding the question
      * Emotional upset that interferes with their thinking
      * Poor health
      * Physical handicap
      * Lack of motivation at time of assessment
      * Lack of testwiseness (understanding how to take tests)

- Lack of confidence leading to evaluation anxiety

B. Possible bias sources that can occur *within the assessment context:*
- Noise distractions
- Poor lighting
- Discomfort
- Lack of rapport with assessor
- Cultural insensitivity by the assessor or within the assessment
- Lack of proper equipment

C. Possible bias sources that can arise from *the assessment itself*
- Directions lacking or vague
- Poorly worded questions
- Poor reproduction of test questions
- Missing information

2. Sources *unique to each assessment method:*

A. Possible sources with *multiple choice tests:*
- There is, in fact, more than one correct or best response
- Incorrect scoring key
- Incorrect bubbling on answer sheet by the respondent
- Clues to the answer in the item or in other items

B. Potential sources with *essay assessments*
- No scoring criteria
- Inappropriate scoring criteria
- Evaluator untrained in applying scoring criteria
- Biased scoring due to stereotyping of respondent
- Insufficient time or patience to read and score carefully
- Students don't know the criteria by which they'll be judged

C. Potential sources *with performance assessment*
- Inappropriate or nonexistent scoring criteria
- Evaluator untrained in applying scoring criteria
- Bias due to stereotypic thinking
- Insufficient time or patience to observe and score carefully
- Unfocused or unclear tasks
- Tasks that don't elicit the correct performance
- Culturally biased tasks
- Students don't know the criteria by which they'll be judged
- Insufficient sample of tasks

D. Possible sources when *using personal communication*
- Not sampling enough performance
- Problems with accurate record keeping
- Language or cultural barriers leading to miscommunication

SUMMARY

Assessment options abound. Some call of questions that are answered right or wrong, while others require observation and professional judgment on the part of the evaluator. If carefully planned and conducted, any of them can provide dependable insights into student learning. Those insights can serve to either verify learning, as when the contribute to the grading process, or to support learning, as when they serve to help students understand and feel in control of their growth.

Effective Communication of Assessment Results

Effective communication conveys useful and accurate information about student achievement from the information gatherer to the intended user(s) in order to help the user decide what to do next. So we need to prepare purposefully, communicate carefully, and follow up to be sure the message was understood.

We already have established that a number of people need access to dependable information about student learning in order to do their jobs. These are important people whose decisions determine student well-being. They need to communicate effectively.

They prepare well by agreeing in advance (between message sender and receiver) precisely what achievement we wish to communicate about, by gathering accurate information about student achievement, by developing a shared vocabulary, and by building an interpersonal environment amenable to honest exchange of information.

They also prepare carefully by anticipating what can go wrong that can keep the message from getting through and by heading those problems off at the pass. We do this by satisfying the certain specific conditions and then by taking the risk of always being open and honest about student learning. This chapter is about those conditions.

One can communicate assessment results in ways that are likely to support learning or to evaluate and just its sufficiency.

The former wants to maximize learning, the latter, grade it. Let's start with grading.

COMMUNICATING ABOUT THE SUFFICIENCY OF LEARNING

If report card grades are to inform students and others about student achievement, then we must clearly and completely articulate and assess the actual achievement standards for which students are to be held accountable. To be effective, we must spell out the valued targets before the grading period begins, lay out in advance an assessment plan to systematically sample those targets, and carry out that plan. While it sounds like there is a great deal of preparation to be done before teaching begins, as it turns out, thoughtful preparation saves a great deal of assessment work during instruction.

Let's analyze an effective and efficient five-step plan for gathering sound and appropriate achievement information for grading purposes.

Step 1: Begin Instruction with the Big Achievement Picture in Mind

To formulate a picture of the valued achievement targets for a given subject over a grading period, gather together all relevant background information: the list of instructional objectives or learning outcomes that is to guide instruction and text materials for the units of instruction to unfold during the grading period. From these, answer the following four questions (they will sound very familiar!):

- What is the subject matter *knowledge* that students are to master? Outline the big ideas and essential concepts that you want students to know and understand. Write them down.

- What patterns of *reasoning* and problem-solving are they to master, if any? Specify each of them in writing.
- What *performance skills*, if any, are students to demonstrate? What things do they need to be able to do? Describe the keys to high quality performance.
- What *products*, if any, are they to create and what are the attributes of a good one? Describe a good one.

Think about these things on a unit-by-unit basis and then map an overall picture of them. Within and across units, develop a sense of the relative importance of these four kinds of targets in your overall expectations. Write down those priorities, with relative emphasis in the form of percentages that add to 100.

As you prepare to present each unit of instruction, you will need to provide your students with (a) student-friendly descriptions of your expectations, and (b) the opportunity to learn to hit each of the kinds of achievement targets you have set out for them. There should be one-to-one correspondence between pre-set targets and subsequent instruction. For each target, you should be able to point to its coverage in your instructional plans.

Step 2: Make an Assessment Plan

How will you assess to accumulate evidence of each student's mastery of those targets? Taken together, the assessments used during the course must help you determine, with confidence, what proportion of the total array of achievement expectations each student has met. Therefore, one must ask, what specific assessments (selected response, essay, perform-ance, or personal communication) will provide an accurate estimate of how much of the required material each student has mastered? When will they be administered? The answers comprise the assessment plan.

You don't need the assessments themselves, not yet. Those come later, as each unit of instruction unfolds. The assessment plan that you start the grading period with needs to satisfy these conditions:

- It needs to foretell each assessment to be conducted for grading, detailing the expected achievement target focus of each, approximately when you expect the assessment to take place, and what assessment method(s) is to be used.
- Each assessment listed in the plan needs to supply an impor-tant piece of the puzzle with respect to the priority targets of the unit and grading period within which it occurs.
- Each assessment must accurately represent the particu-lar targets(s) it is supposed to depict (i.e., each must be a sound assessment according to previously stated quality standards).
- The full array of assessments conducted across units over the entire grading period must accurately determine the proportion of your expectations that each student has attained.
- The entire assessment plan must involve a reasonable assess-ment workload for both you and your students.

These conditions may be easier to meet than you think. The key to practical success here is to gather the fewest pos-sible assessments for grading and still generate an accurate estimate of performance. With well-planned, strategic assessments, one can generate accurate estimates of achievement very economically.

Avoid the shotgun approach to grading, where one just gathers a huge array of graded student work over the course of the grading period, feeling that surely somewhere, somehow, some of it will reflect some of the valued targets. While this may be true in part, this approach is at best inefficient. Plan ahead and minimize assessment work.

A Note of Caution:

Remember that we can assess to diagnose student needs, provide students with practice performing or evaluating their own performance, and help students track their growth as a result of instruction. In fact, sometimes we can assess just to boost student confidence by helping them see themselves growing. Generally, it's a bad idea to factor into the report card grade assessments intended for practice. Just as football teams practice a great deal before being held accountable for their performance, so too should students be given the opportunity for guided practice with descriptive feedback before being held accountable in a grading sense. In other words, we should not grade students during the time when they are evaluating their own needs or trying to discover the keys to their own success. Practice assessments are for polishing skills, overcoming problems, and fine tuning performance. We shouldn't grade students when they are trying to learn from their mistakes. Students need time simply to muck around with new learnings, time to discover through risk-free experimentation, time to fail and learn from it without the shadow of evaluative judgment.

You might be saying, "If I don't assign a grade and have it count toward the grade, students won't take it seriously and won't do it!" Trust me: once students come to understand that they do get to practice with assessments along the way to competence and once they learn that formative feedback really helps, and once the begin to watch their competence increasing, they will practice if they need to. Once they reach the desired level of mastery in formative practice, they can decide that more practice is no long necessary. They can be in control of this. But they must know that performance on graded assessments is what counts for their grade. By the time they reach the college level, our students must learn to take responsibility for developing their own sense of control over their success. This way of thinking about "first we practice and get good at it and then we demonstrate success" really boosts student confidence, motivation, engagement and ultimate achievement.

Step 3: Actual Assessments

In each case where you have knowledge and reasoning targets to assess via selected response or essay assessments, you need to devise those specific assessments around precisely defined categories of knowledge and kinds of reasoning. You can capture these in lists of objectives, tables of specification, propositions, and finally the test exercises themselves, which you may assemble into assignments, quizzes, and tests.

When assessing performance skill and product outcomes, you need to assemble performance criteria, tasks to elicit performance, and rating scales or checklists. Each component assessment fills in part of your big picture.

All assessments must align exactly with your vision of student competence. Although you may develop some in advance, to save time later, you may develop others during instruction. I know this sounds like a great deal of work, but remember these five important facts:

- This sharply targeted grading approach is not nearly as much work as the shotgun approach.
- It affords the conscientious instructor a great deal more peace of mind. When our students obviously are succeeding, we know we have been successful.
- In between your periodic assessments for grading purposes, students can play key roles in the use of practice assessments, thus turning nearly all of that assessment time and energy into productive learning.
- Student motivation to learn is likely to increase; "no surprises, no excuses" leads to a success orientation.
- The plans and assessments you develop now remain intact for you to use or adapt the next time you teach the same material, and the time after that. Thus, development costs are spread out over the useful life of your plan and its associated assessments.

Step 4: A Composite Index of Achievement

At the end of the grading period, your records should tell you about each student's performance in meeting your expectations. The question is, how do you get a grade out of all of this information?

Rely on a consistent computational sequence for all students that you can reproduce later should you need to explain the process or revise a grade. Such a sequence helps to control for your personal biases, which may either inappropriately inflate or deflate a grade for reasons unrelated to actual achievement.

Please note that I am not opposed to a role for professional judgment in grading. As we established in earlier chapters, that role comes in the design and administration of the assessments used to gather information about student achievement. We need to minimize subjectivity when combining indicators of achievement for grading purposes. Let the evidence speak for itself.

To derive a meaningful grade from several records of achievement, again, *each piece of information gathered should indicate the proportion of the targets each student has mastered.* So, if we combine them all, we should obtain an estimate of the proportion mastered for the total grading period. Think of each assessment as a part of the achievement mosaic Two relatively simple ways to achieve it are the percent method and the total points method.

Percent Method. Convert each student's performance on each contributing assessment into a percent of required learning targets mastered. If you convert everything to the same percent scale, then both record keeping and later computation become much simpler.

If the individual assessment results recorded as percentages are averaged across all assessments for a whole grading period, then the result should indicate the proportion of the total array of expectations for that grading period that each student has mastered. In effect, translating each score into a percent places all on the same scale for averaging purposes and permits you to combine them in an easily interpreted manner, in terms of intended targets. With this procedure, if you wish to give greater weight to some assessment results than to others, you can accomplish this by multiplying those scores by their weight before adding them into the overall computation.

With this system of record keeping and grade computation based on percent of learning targets mastered, if students receive a list of expectations at the outset, they can know their status at any point in time in relation to expectations.

Total Points Method. Another way to combine information is to define the target for a grading period in terms of a total number of points. Students who earn all or most of the points demonstrate mastery of all or most of the valued targets and earn a high grade.

In this case, each individual assessment contributes a certain number of points to the total. If you carefully plan this so the points earned on each assessment reflect their fair share of the big picture, then at the end of the grading period you can simply add up each student's points and determine what percentage of the total each student earned. That percentage of total points, then, represents the proportion of valued targets attained. Just remember that the assessments that result in the largest number of points will contribute the most to the determination of the final grade.

This fact makes differential weighting possible. Just be sure that you assign a large number of points to those learning targets that represent your highest priorities and, therefore, to your assessments (such as final exams or large projects) that cover the largest proportions of the valued targets and fewer points to the assessments (such as daily assignments) that are narrower in focus.

Some Practical Advice

Unless you carefully develop and summarize assessment results, they may be misleading about the proportion of the total achievement picture that students have mastered. Here are some guidelines to think about when being careful:

Use the Most Current Information. Let's say your strategic assessment plan includes five unit assessments and a comprehensive final exam that covers the entire set of targets for the grading period. And, say a particular student starts slowly, scoring very low on the first two unit assessments, but gains momentum and attains a perfect score on the comprehensive final exam, revealing, in effect, subsequent mastery of the material covered in those first two unit assessments.

The key grading question is this: Which piece of information provides the most accurate depiction of that student's real achievement at the end of the grading period, the final exam score or that score averaged with all five unit tests? If the final is truly comprehensive in its coverage of your essential learning targets, averaging it with the results of earlier assessments will result in misleading information.

If students demonstrate achievement at any time that, in effect, renders past assessment information invalid, then you must drop the former assessment from the record and replace it with the new—even if the new information reflects a lower level of achievement. To do otherwise is to misrepresent that achievement.

Grade on Status versus Improvement. An issue many teachers struggle with is whether a grade should reflect a student's achievement status at the end of the grading period or improvement over time. The resolution of this important issue lies in understanding the immense difficulties we face here.

If *improvement* means that those who gain more over time get higher grades, students who happen to arrive knowing less have an advantage. Is that fair to those who arrive knowing more? Besides, to grade on improvement, you need to establish a baseline by conducting a comprehensive pre-assessment of students on all relevant outcomes for that grading period. We are seldom able to pre-assess to this level of detail. And even if you could, you would face challenging statistical problems in dealing effectively with the undependable "gain scores" that would result.

For these reasons, grades should reflect each student's end status in attaining the pre-specified targets in that classroom during the grading period just completed.

Borderline Cases. Another common problem arises when a particular student's academic average is literally right on the borderline between two grades and you just don't know which way to go. Some teachers allow factors unrelated to achievement such as the students attitude or apparent level of effort to push the grade one way or the other. A better way to determine such grades is to collect one or two significant pieces of achievement data during grading that overlap other assessments, thus double checking previous information about achievement. Hold these assessments in reserve, don't factor them into your grades. Then, if you need "swing votes," use them to help you decide which grade to assign. This keeps unrelated factors out of both the grading decision and the communication system.

Dealing with Cheating. Let's say a student cheats on a test and, as punishment, is given a zero in the grade book, to be averaged with other assessments to determine the semester grade. The problem is that the zero almost surely misrepresents that student's real level of achievement. To prevent this, one must separate the grade and the discipline for cheating. Retest the student to determine real levels of achievement and enter that retest score into the grade book. Punish cheating in some manner other than falsifying the achievement record.

Awarding "Extra Credit." It is not uncommon for some faculty to strive to encourage extra effort on the part of their students by offering extra credit opportunities. Be very careful here. If grades are to reflect achievement, deliver the consistent message that *the more you learn, the better your grade.* If extra credit work is specifically designed to provide dependable information that students have learned more, then it should influence the grade assigned. But if students come to believe that merely doing the work, whether or not it results in greater learning, is sufficient to attain a higher grade, then it is counterproductive.

Prior Notice. Be sure all students know and understand in advance the procedures you will use to compute their grades. What assessments will you conduct, when, and how will you factor each into your grading? What are students' timelines, deadlines, and important responsibilities? If students know their responsibilities up front, they have a good chance of succeeding.

The Bottom Line. Grades must convey as accurate a picture of a student's real achievement as possible. Any practice that has the effect of misrepresenting actual achievement of agreed upon standards is unacceptable.

Step 5: Converting Achievement to Grades

How does one convert a composite index of student achievement into an accurate report card grade? Traditionally, we have accomplished this in one of two ways: (1) grade in terms of preset performance standards or (2) assign the grade based on to the student's place in the rank order of class members. In an era of achievement or performance-driven education, only the first option makes sense. Let's explore each and see why.

Grading with Preset Standards. Grading in terms of preset standards says upfront, here are the assessments that represent the achievement targets to be mastered; score at this level on them and this is the grade you will receive. A set of percentage cutoff scores is fixed and all who score within certain ranges receive that designated grade: 90–100 = A, 80–89 = B, etc.

If two important conditions are met, this method maximizes the opportunity for success for students. Those conditions are (1) that students possess the prerequisites to master the required material, and (2) that assessments accurately represent the targets on which you will base the grade.

One advantage of this system is that the meaning of the grade is clearly couched in the attainment of intended achievement targets. Another is that it is computationally simple; you need only know how to compute percentages and averages. Still another strength is that grades can work effectively in the context of a continuous progress curriculum. As students master prerequisites for later, more advanced work, as indicated by high grades, teachers can know that they are ready for the next stage. A fourth advantage is that grading in terms of preset standards increases the possibility that all students can succeed, if they achieve. And finally, from the instructor's perspective, if one becomes more effective over time, greater student success will be reflected in a greater proportion of higher grades—for anyone who has committed her or his career to teaching, this is a very good thing…

Grading "On a Curve". The tactic of assigning grades based on students' place in the rank order of achievement scores within a class is commonly referred to as "grading on a curve." In its classic application, the teacher uses the composite index of achievement for each student to rank students from the highest to the lowest. Then, counting from the top, the teacher counts off 7 percent of the students on the list.

These students receive As. Then the next 24 percent receive Bs, and so on down to the bottom 7 percent of students, who are assigned Fs.

Another variation on this method is to tally how many students attained each score and then to graph that distribution to find natural gaps between groups of scores that appear to permit division into groups of students to whom you can then assign different grades.

These ranking methods have the strength of yielding a grade that is interpreted in terms of group performance. They also have the effect of promoting competition among students: Students will know that their challenge is to outscore the others.

But in a context in which high achievement is the goal, the limitations of such a system become far more prominent than the strengths. The percentage of students receiving each grade is not a matter of science. Again, the cutoffs are arbitrary, and once grades are assigned and recorded on the transcript, no user of that grade information will necessarily know or understand the system of cutoffs used by the grader.

Besides, it's not clear what group should be ranked for grading purposes. Is it all students in the same class at the same time? In the same college? In the same semester or year? Over the years? The answers to these questions can have major implications for the grade a student receives and how others interpret the grades assigned. For instance, if a student happens to fall into an extremely capable cohort, the results might be vastly different from how they would be if that same student just happens to be part of a generally lower-achieving group. So issues of fairness come into play.

Further, this system produces grades that are unrelated to real achievement. A class could, in fact, learn very little but the grade distribution could still convey the appearance that all had performed as expected. In other words, in a high-achieving group, some who actually learned a great deal but scored below the highest achievers might be doomed to receive a low grade.

And again, from your point of view as a teacher, even if your instruction improves markedly over the years and helps more and more students master the important material, the distribution of grades will appear unchanged. That would frustrate anyone!

Teachers who develop success-oriented partnerships with students have no use for grading on a curve. They know they are not the best teacher they can be until every student attains an A by demonstrating the highest possible achievement on rigorous, high-quality assessments.

COMMUNICATION FOR THE PURPOSE OF SUPPORTING LEARNING

Assessments conducted to support learning should yield results that serve to keep students informed of and feeling in control of their academic success. When these assessments FOR learning are in play, it's best to keep the grade book closed. Students need to feel that these are intended as learning experiences. Use separate summative assessments at grading time. Keep them separate. If keeping records of both, rely on separate information management systems.

Think of a classroom driven by a continuous array of assessments for practice, most being conducted and used by students themselves to watch themselves grow—always under

113

the watchful eye of their instructor. These, then, need to be punctuated by periodic assessments whose purpose is to verify learning—always announced well in advance, so students know when it's time to demonstrate competence so others can see how to help them. Everyone involved needs to see the relationship between these two purposes for assessment—everything counts, some for practice and some for grading. There should be no surprises and no excuses. When the results count for practice, special communication tactics become important.

Results that Support Learning

Previously, we established that, when used in support of learning, we need evidence that tracks student progress up the scaffolding of knowledge, reasoning, skill, or product proficiencies that lead to each instructor's definition of competence. In this kind of assessment to support learning scenario, one must develop an assessment map that reflects the learning progressions of the curriculum so instructor and students can anticipate when each assessment will happened and how its results will help them. As their teachers, we must understand that feedback that is most likely to help satisfies these criteria:

- Focuses on attributes of the work rather than on attributes of the student
- Is descriptive of the work; how to do better next time
- Clearly understood by the learner
- In bit-sized chunks–helpful, but does not overwhelm
- Arrives in time to inform the learning

But in contexts in which assessment serves to support learning, we want the assessment map, information management,

114

and communication systems to involve students so that the evidence reveals to them the change in their achievement over time. Part of the professor's instructional job is to be sure they learn to understand the changes in their own academic capabilities as they grow.

Record Keeping

When using assessment to support learning, one wants to retain a detailed description of achievement, perhaps including actual samples of student work. This application of assessment is not about accountability or report card grades. We want students to watch themselves improving over time—to see evidence in their results that learning targets they could not hit before they are hitting now. They might maintain a working folder or portfolio of evidence to include periodic self-reflections by students on changes in their own achievement. In this case, the records are the students to keep under the watchful eye of and consultation with their teacher. They build the evidence that tells the story of their own journey to success over time. The richer the descriptive detail of assessment results, the sharper will be the students' ability to focus on critical improvements needed in their work.

SUMMARY

We assess, in part, to gather information about student achievement so that information can be used to facilitate instructional decision making. If one is to make sound decisions, one needs accurate information arising from quality assessments. Quality assessments arise from a clear vision of the learning target students are to hit. Once one knows the information needs of the decision maker(s) and the target, then and only then can one create an assessment to fit that context. Once developed and administered, that assessment will evidence of the level of student achievement. The assessor's communication challenge is to deliver that evidence into the hands of its intended user in a timely and understandable manner. Communication vehicles and options abound. But to be effective, the communication process must satisfy certain conditions. Message sender and receiver must share a vision of the learning target and a common language for communicating results. Again, the evidence must be accurate, and the channels of communication must be open for the message to get through, be heard and be acted upon. When these conditions are satisfied, assessment results can either support or verify learning, depending on the context.

Figure 6.1 provides a concise summary of the assessment competencies post-secondary faculty must bring to the classroom assessment process in order to be ready to fulfill their ongoing assessment responsibilities.

Figure 6.1
Indicators of Sound Assessment Practice
in the College Classroom

1. Why Assess? **Assessment Processes and Results Serve Clear and Appropriate Purposes**	a. Instructor understands who classroom assessment users are and their information needs. b. Understands the assessment and student motivation and can use assessment experiences to maximize motivation. c. Can use classroom assessment processes and results formatively to support learning (assessment *for* learning). d. Can use classroom assessment results in a summative manner to verify learning (assessment *of* learning) at a particular point in time.
2. Assess What? **Assessments Reflect Clear and Valued Student Learning Targets**	a. Instructor has clear classroom learning targets for students anchored to standards b. Understands the differences among the various types of learning targets c. Focuses learning targets on the most important things students need to know and be able to do d. Has plan for assessing all key learning targets over time.
3. Assess How? **Learning Targets Are Translated into Assessments That Yield Accurate Results**	a. Instructor understands each of the various assessment methods. b. Can choose assessment methods that match intended learning targets. c. Designs assessments that fit the purpose/target context. d. Samples learning appropriately in their assessments. e. Creates sound exercises and scoring schemes of all types well. f. Avoids bias that distorts results.
4. Communicate How? **Assessment Results Are Managed Well and Communicated Effectively**	a. Instructor records and summarizes assessment information so as to accurately reflects student learning. b. Selects the best reporting option (grades, narratives, portfolios, conferences) for each context (learning targets and users). c. Interprets and use test results correctly. d. Effectively communicates assessment results to students. e. Effectively communicates assessment results to a variety of audiences
5. Involve Students How? **Students Are Involved in Their Own Assessment**	a. Instructor makes learning targets clear to students. b. Involves students in practice assessment development and use as appropriate. b. Involves students in assessing, tracking, and setting goals for their own learning. c. Involves students in communicating about their own learning.

Made in the USA
Lexington, KY
06 February 2015